Praise for
Shepreneur

Kristin Cripps has written a bible for women wanting everything they can get from life on their own steam. I especially appreciated her messages around female empowerment—that not only can women do it all by themselves, but they should. I plan on sharing this book with every young woman in my life to inspire them to stop waiting for life to hand them a thing and instead go out and get it, girl!

Ali Razi |
founder & CEO, Banc Certified Merchant Services

Kristin's book, *Shepreneur*, surprised me in a good way. At first, I thought it would be another book about how life handed her lemonade. Nope! She did it all by herself. The power of tenacity is evidenced over and again in Kristin's humorous stories. She didn't give up no matter what happened. I was impressed by even when she encountered some pretty significant financial challenges, she just dug in and worked even harder. She never gave up—and neither will the entrepreneurs who read it!

Mark Nureddine |
CEO, Bull Outdoor Products; best-selling author of Pocket Mentor

If you want to start a business. If you want to become a millionaire. If you want to be inspired. Read *Shepreneur*. Kristin shares her life experience in a real, raw, and attainable way. When you read how she went from A (broke bartender) to Z (real estate mogul), you'll see how you can get there too. Great stories. Great read. Great book.

Steffani Fort LeFevour |
happiness coach

It's very inspirational to read the backstory of a how-to gal who "started from the bottom." In her book, *Shepreneur*, Kristin Cripps shows us in a lighthearted and humorous way how she massaged, served, bartended, and "real-estated" her way to millionaire status before the age of thirty! I just love that she stated many times that if she can do it, so can anyone else. Kristin shows us that financial freedom is obtainable to everyone!

Deborah Murtagh |
weight loss coach

I completely enjoyed reading this book. Kristin's story is straight to the point just like I like them. I love how she provided a lot of examples for taking control of a life that I can start implementing in my own life. My favorite part is learning her story and how she built a successful career from scratch. I will strongly recommend this book to my girlfriends who are seeking inspiration from a true powerhouse!

Ruqaya Kalla |
entrepreneur, holistic healer,
NLP trainer, personal growth coach

Kristin Cripps is a great storyteller. This book is a perfect gift for anyone thinking about starting a business or just wanting to be inspired by a badass businesswoman (or man, for that matter). I really liked that she told her story, warts and all, and showed how—despite what life threw her way—she just kept on climbing up. We could all learn a lot from her can-do mindset and attitude!

Alfio Bardolla |
financial coach, author

I would highly recommend *Shepreneur* to any woman or man who seeks a confidence boost in their career or someone who plans on elbow-greasing their way up the ladder. Kristin's funny tale of mistakes made and lessons learned prove that anyone can do what she's done! No more excuses—get out and make it happen for yourself by yourself!

Jason Goldberg |
author of *Prison Break*

Most business books for me are difficult to read and I usually end up putting them down for something more entertaining. However, this book combined learning and humor in a way that made me want to rush out and start buying real estate and travelling more. I love how the author empowers females to dominate the work place, even reading this from a man's perspective. She is humble about how it took her a few tries to make it, but with hard work and dedication she did it. A true boss!

Jeff Hays |
producer, Jeff Hays Films

Love, love, love this book! Kristin is real and approachable and speaks a language that everyone can understand. There are already too many books out there that speak down to those trying to learn the ropes. Not Kristin. She's right there in the trenches with you and inspiring you to put some elbow grease in it and hustle for your dreams. I recommend reading this book again and again!

Tony White |
executive chairman, enChoice, Inc.

SHEPRENEUR

I Can. I Will. Watch Me!

Life Lessons for the Determined Female Entrepreneur

Kristin Cripps

Leaders
Press

Cover by Dalchand Sharma

ISBN (pbk) 978-1-943386-79-6
ISBN (ebook) 978-1-943386-80-2
Library of Congress Control Number: 2020902536

Dedication

I'm dedicating this book to everyone who had a part in my upbringing. I know that seems super vague, but I always try to see the best in everything and everyone.

Thanks to my dad and stepmom for showing me how to be a little powerhouse and not bringing me up like a spoiled only child. You taught me the value of hard work. You knew no one would mess with me and that I could conquer anything I desired—not like telling a five-year-old you can be whatever you want when you grow up, but you genuinely meant it.

Props (yes, I'm giving *props* because I'm not a fancy person who needs to use excessively elaborate words that aren't used in real life) to my mom for being a single mom and driving me all over Timbuktu for dance competitions and putting up with my stubbornness and shenanigans.

Along those same lines, I'm thankful to my stepfather for being more like a sibling and kicking me under the table and showing me the food in his mouth when Mom looked away, and for having someone else to blame things on since there were no siblings in the house.

A special thanks to Omi—although not with us in the flesh—for being my bestie every other weekend, for our imagination extravaganzas, for our super unsafe car fun, and for being the best grandparent ever! (I had seven grandparents, so that's a lot of competition.)

You are all loved tremendously and very dear to my heart!

On a sidenote, I dedicate this book to my worst friend ever,

Shepreneur

Melony (who is not really the worst—still, we call her that because she can be a wee bit crusty), for telling me that her mortgage was less than my rent and inevitably getting me into the real estate market.

Contents

Introduction

Did you know that everyone is a millionaire?

I bet you're making a WTF face right now. I draw my eyebrows on crooked all the time (not on purpose), but maybe as you read these first few lines, you're making a funny eyebrow face.

It's true: you either have a million dollars, or you have a million excuses. Believe it or not, hells to the yes—that's true. So which kind of millionaire do you want to be?

I know I don't want to be a millionaire of excuses—nope, zip to the zero. (Anyone who tells you that's the stupidest thing they've ever heard is the second type of millionaire.)

We all know there are tons of books about how to make money, be a better person, and visualize your ideal life into reality. Those stories are hard to believe if you're sitting on some ratty old couch reading a book about someone who takes their ten thousand employees on annual trips to the author's private island.

Well, this isn't that kind of book because *my* lifestyle isn't out of reach for anybody.

My parents didn't hand me anything. For back-to-school shopping, we went to Value Village or Goodwill, where I would get one shirt, one pair of pants, and one jacket, which would total somewhere around fifteen to eighteen dollars.

Shepreneur

When I was fifteen years old, if you had told me that I would be a millionaire before I was thirty, I would have made that funny WTF eyebrow face. I was one year away from leaving home to make my way in the world, and like most kids that age, I thought I knew everything.

So I moved from my mom and stepdad's place to a cockroach-infested apartment, where I learned how much money life costs and that I didn't have that money. That was the first of three times I contemplated stripping. I found the most popular club in Hamilton, got in with my fake ID, and spoke to the owner.

He looked me up and down and said, "You can start tomorrow," but he never asked me how old I was. I was sixteen—old enough to have a job, but not old enough to have that kind of a job. When I walked outside, I saw a man with a snake around his neck—not a little garden snake, but a huge snake about the size of my thigh. (Okay, I'm exaggerating—the snake was the size of my calf, but still.)

I remember thinking how scary and creepy the man looked, and I knew I didn't want to work there as I blubbered like a child all the way back to my apartment.

So I passed on the stripping job (you're welcome, Dad). I worked a lot of hours, but by following a path of common sense (which I'm going to share with you), I was a millionaire before my thirtieth birthday. My success was no accident, and there was no clear path to it, either, except my hustle.

This book won't tell you how to become a real estate mogul (that's my second book, insert shameless plug here), but I'll share some advice I learned along the way that will help you on your journey, no matter what you're planning.

People don't become excellent accidentally; they work for it in all aspects of the word. And work hard, I did: three jobs at a time. I had saved $85,000 by the time I was nineteen years old, and then I found my way into the world of real estate.

I know you're making that eyebrow face again. I mean, who the fuck saves $85,000 during their teenage years?

Well, I did. And if I can save some money, so can you, even if you're way past being a teenager.

I want to help people—specifically women—become success stories. This isn't a *woo-woo* book—far from it. But I do want to help you figure out what makes you happy and identify your deepest dreams that truly light you up.

Step 1 to success: You have to know what you want.

Think about what makes you so happy that you would do it for free. I have heard women say countless times that they want their kids to have the best lives possible and live out all their dreams and so forth.

But wait—what about *mom's* dreams?

Having dreams and making them happen isn't being selfish. If your kids see you going after what you want and sometimes failing but getting back up and achieving, then you're a damn good role model.

Step 2 to success: You have to know what's running on autopilot in your head.

I want you to become aware of all the garbage, bullshit stories, negative thoughts, and self-doubts in your head. I want you to become informed about your daily thoughts and habits so that you can align your life with your truth and act with authenticity.

- ❏ Is what you're regularly doing aligning with your dreams?
- ❏ If not, how can you design your life for precisely what you want?
- ❏ When you think of what you want, whether that's a relationship or a job, what are you looking for?
- ❏ Why do you want it?
- ❏ What will your life be like if you get it?
- ❏ What are the steps you can take every day to move toward what you want?

Step 3 to success: What you think and do every day— not the actions of others—is what defines you.

I'm no guru, and I'm not preaching. I'm telling you the truth, whether you're ready to hear it or not (but I have a sneaking suspicion you are, or you wouldn't be reading this book).

I don't like it when people blame others. I can't even give examples of what blame looks like because that's how much I dislike that mentality. But just because I don't like that mentality doesn't mean I think you're a terrible person if you're still playing the blame game.

Become aware of how you're using blame and excuses. Then you can take steps to change your mindset and habits to get you to a healthier place in life and consequently to get what you want.

Stop blaming other people and things, and take action on how you can change yourself. If you keep waiting for a good life to happen accidentally or for someone to give it to you, there's a staggeringly high chance you're going to be waiting until you end up in your coffin.

(In other words, it's not happening. I hate to break it to you, but I will.)

It's kind of like wanting to win the lottery but never buying a ticket or wanting to lose a hundred pounds but never hitting the gym or eating healthy food. It's a head-shaker to me, but I see it all the time. I don't like shame, so I never tell myself that I'm wrong or stupid because I did so many particularly crazy things. I want the same thing for you. I prefer positive self-affirmation, learning, and moving forward.

So why should you read a book written by a former bartender and massage therapist turned real estate mogul?

The truth is that I'm just a regular person. (The word *mogul* kind of makes me laugh.) I don't have a fancy degree, never even been to university. I grew up with my single mom; we couch-surfed for a while and at times were on public assistance.

Shepreneur

I didn't grow up on the "right" side of the tracks around affluent people or knowledgeable, experienced investors. My mom rented until I was ten years old, and then she and my stepdad moved in together. My grandma rented until she passed, so I didn't grow up with the advice that buying real estate and investments was the way to go.

A fellow recently asked me, "How do you feel when people ask you how you became successful or when they ask you for advice? Do you feel flattered? Annoyed? What crosses your mind?"

I told him that I find those kinds of questions a little odd because I don't think I did anything secret or out of the ordinary. I consider myself to be a regular person, and I didn't do anything that's not straightforward and doable by anybody else.

The only difference is that I actually did it instead of sitting back and watching other people do it.

On that note, let's get this party started—not because life is one big party, but because life is such a trip and a wild ride and guess what, you're in charge!

Ready to live your best life?

Let's go!

Chapter 1

Independence

I Can! I Will! Watch Me!

It's never too early or too late to seize your independence.

This book is for you, so it won't be my straight-up biography. You'll see that I'm just an ordinary person and that my story of success could easily be yours too.

When I was two years old (I promise this will be relevant), I attended a nursery school as many children do. A little boy started picking on me, and when my dad arrived at the end of the day to pick me up, he wanted to save me. He told the supervisor he wanted to have a chat with the little fellow and his parents. But the supervisor said, "No, leave Kristin be. She will be just fine, believe me."

Less than ten seconds later, I'd had enough and hit the little boy over the head multiple times with a plastic phone. (I guess I wasn't going to take anyone's shit, even from a young age.) I'm neither a violent person nor one who condones violence, and I have never been in a fight in my life. I've never been put on detention or called to the principal's office, but sometimes you have to stand up for yourself.

Two years later, again at day care, a different boy thought he was stronger than me. Well, this time, it turned out that he was.

Shepreneur

Our little wrestling match resulted in a greenstick fracture to my arm (wasn't broken all the way through) and a dislocated shoulder. I ended up in the hospital with a phone call to my not-very-impressed mother.

That brings me to my point: you have to keep seizing your independence. It isn't a onetime deal where you grab it, and you're the queen of the mountain, and you retire on your throne. Life's a continual learning process, and the playing field will always be shifting.

My mom signed me up for T-ball when I was five years old. I remember going to bat and peering out from under my helmet at all the other players in the field. They looked like teenagers, and they were foaming at the mouth. (At least that's how it seemed to me.)

So I didn't hit the ball. Instead, I sat down and said that my tummy hurt. I never played another game. Wonder what would have happened if I had continued to face my fears at that early age?

Speaking of independence, way too many times, people ask me who "helped" get me where I am. The answer is that no one helped me; I did it all by myself, and so can you. Most of us have had a teacher or a friend or family member or someone who believed in us or encouraged us along the way, and yes, I was the beneficiary of such kindness.

But the hustle was all mine.

Rather than being influenced by other people to get where I am, I was more influenced by not wanting to feel stuck. I knew there was more I wanted to do than continue waitressing or bartending my entire life. (Hugs to all my girls who are still in it. You ladies are resilient and put up with so much shit. I couldn't do it. Keep kicking ass and shots all around.) I wanted to pursue a different path.

I believe that if you strip the money away from something you're doing, you should still enjoy what you do. Making money is a big part of my real estate career, but there's a lot of it that I genuinely enjoy. If I didn't enjoy it, I wouldn't have tried so hard—and probably wouldn't have succeeded the way I did.

Enjoyment kept me hanging in there when things were tough.

For example, I bought a duplex, and three weeks after purchasing it, *nine inches* of water flooded the basement apartment. Not ideal. Happy house-warming Kristin: Voila! Water, water, and more water! The person I was dating at the time said, "Sell it, and pay off your Visa. You're in way over your head."

Fortunately, I'd learned not to listen to other people by then, so I didn't sell it. Instead, I chose to fix it for $12,000 and sold it six years after purchasing it for $285,000 more than I bought it for.

Woohoo! Queen of the mountain again (until the next time).

Too many people rely on others to give them what they want. I have never understood that mentality and the lack of desire not to do something for themselves. I always wanted to do it all on my own (well, except for T-ball). If I was going to be set for life, it was going to be because of my hard work, determination, and brains. I wanted to climb the ladder of success using my skills. I didn't want my success to result from handouts from anyone, which brings me to my next point.

No job is beneath you, so don't be "above" something.

As a kid, I babysat for a family with two kids and charged them $4 an hour. I wouldn't hang out at their house; I'd take the kids out to different places. For example, the kids had never taken a bus, so we rode the bus to the movies or to the mall where we'd take funny photos in the photo booth. I wanted to be fun for the kids. I didn't want them to say, "Oh no, the babysitter is coming!" I wanted them to be excited, "The babysitter is coming!"

I wasn't very good at saving money back then. If I made $40, I'd probably spend $25 to $30 on the kids, as I enjoyed showing them a good time. When I taught acro dancing and ballet as a kid, I made $3 an hour. (When kids are not yet fourteen years old, the employer can pay whatever they want under the table. My mom took a photocopy of my first paycheque from Ensemble Dance Studio to Kristin Cripps, which was $12.)

My first real job was at a train and bus station where the owner charged people 50¢ to use the restroom if they didn't buy anything from her. People would complain that a train station should have a free bathroom, but the station was a privately run business, so it was the owner's choice as to how she wanted to run it.

Her patrons were mad because they had to pay to pee, so they took it out (literally) on the bathroom stalls. I think the sign pissed people off (yeah, pun intended), so they would purposely miss the toilet. Guess who had to clean it up? Yep, me. It was a disgusting job, but I didn't complain because it was a paycheque. I wasn't above it, as that was just part of the job.

The station had a little cafe, so don't feel sorry for me and think that I was just cleaning pee all day. I made egg, tuna, and chicken salad sandwiches, and soup and chili. Also, we sold chocolate bars, chips, and magazines. Then we'd make all the food for the trains that would pass through from Toronto to North Bay.

I cleaned the bathrooms and picked up the cigarette butts and did anything else that needed to be done. The station was two doors away from my dad's office, so he would drive me to work. He'd go home afterward because he finished earlier than I did, then he'd come back later and pick me up. I was fourteen years old and made $6.40 an hour.

The lady who hired me initially didn't think I would work out. She felt that since I was a doctor's daughter, I wasn't going to be a good worker. (I should mention that my dad is a doctor, but I promise his career choice has zero, zip, zilch to do with my success. However, he did tell me bedtime stories with some good life lessons.)

Well, the owner agreed to hire me, and she probably expected I'd be some lazy, spoiled brat. But once I started working, she saw that I worked: I cleaned the toilets and mopped the floors and had everything done ahead of time. I didn't feel above the job.

Shepreneur

There was another girl working at the station who read the gossipy magazines all day and didn't do any work, but I've never been that type of person. I worked twelve to sixteen-hour days when the night train was late, which was pretty much every other day.

When you have that kind of job, you can learn many life lessons. I believe there's always a lesson, a story, or someone you're supposed to meet in every scenario. Thinking positively and striving in those jobs pays tenfold in other and often unexpected ways.

Maybe you decide to go back to school because if that's your only career option, you know you'd soon be miserable. Perhaps you learn recipes and become a great cook. You learn to deal with angry people being rude to you because they're late for their bus or train. You learn to deal with other people in other environments as you climb your ladder to success.

Most of us have to work our way up. We don't automatically land at the top with a snap of our fingers. Many people want the magic pill or the secret button that creates success without putting in the work. But you'll feel much more appreciative if you've done all the heavy lifting yourself, and you will know how hard specific jobs can be.

We're all people; we're all human. So if you're still a millionaire of excuses, I suggest you hop off your high horse and work your way up. If you've already worked your way up, then more power to you and feel free to get back up on your horse and ride on.

I've taken jobs in the past that I knew weren't my endgame. For example, I worked at a nightclub where I had to dance on the bar and get the female patrons to join me. The ladies would hop on the bar and start dancing too, and this was the owner's plan to attract guys to the bar to watch the girls: they would buy drinks from the male bartenders standing below, and then we would all split the tips.

One day, we were told by the nightclub's management that we were having our pictures taken.

When I asked, "For what?" I was told, "You'll see."

I learned that our photos were made into large stickers and placed above the urinals in the men's bathroom. Incidentally, this happened to be the last place I wanted my picture hung since I was trying to make it in real estate at the time. I didn't want people meeting me to look at a property and ask, "Whoa! Aren't you that girl from the bar bathroom?" Um, no, thank you!

(That's one of the many reasons I never put my face on my "for sale" signs: I didn't want people recognizing me as that "bar girl.")

But I needed to keep that job back then. If I said anything about the pee sign (or anything else, to be honest), one of three things would happen: they would give me the worst bar, no shifts at all, or I'd be straight-up fired—and my face would remain in the men's bathroom. So speaking up wasn't an option.

Sometimes you have to suck it up and not let things disturb your realm. Pick your battles, as the saying goes. (My picture stayed for years in that bathroom after I left until, thankfully, a friend of mine took it down for me.)

Shepreneur

I once dated and lived with someone who hadn't worked in eight months. I would give them a variety of jobs and fix-ups at my rental properties to help make them feel like they were contributing. I didn't want to pile on the shame and make them feel like a freeloader.

One of my clients offered a job as a local school janitor to my live-in friend. This job had set hours, benefits, and vacation. If my memory serves me correctly, it paid $25 an hour when the minimum wage was just over $10 an hour.

It was a great gig, and they could be home every day at a decent hour with no commute. I don't mean to disrespect any janitors out there, but the person I was dating didn't want to take the job—not even until a more desirable job came up. I was told, "I will never clean fucking toilets for a living. Are you kidding me? You think I would do that?"

Remembering all the toilets I cleaned in my life, I asked, "I'm sorry, but do you have something else to do to earn money? Because the last time I checked, money didn't grow on trees. You need to eat, pay for a car and the clothes on your body, and put a roof over your head."

Some people feel they are too entitled to do any jobs that they think are below them. In my opinion, a job is a job: suck it up, do it, and do the best you can, or you're never going to excel at any position. When someone wants to hire you at a better job somewhere else, you won't have the drive and determination to go there. And that's if they even want you.

Keep your drains plugged, keep the place clean, and keep your lights on.

Strange metaphorical advice, but true.

As I mentioned, I left home at an early age. Although seizing your independence is the subject of this chapter, the truth is that I went out on my own because, as a typical teenager, I wasn't getting on well with my mom and stepdad. I thought it would be easy breezy to live on my own, so I rushed out to get an apartment, thinking that living on my own was going to be smooth sailing.

My dad offered to move me to the tiny town where he lived, but it was too small for me. Only 15,000 people live there now, and that's with two decades of population growth. To go from a city of 550,000 people to a small village was not something any self-respecting teenager wanted to do. I didn't want to move to the middle of nowhere, although my dad would happily have taken me.

My dad came down with me to look for apartments because nobody wanted to rent to a sixteen-year-old, so he had to cosign the lease with me.

But the apartment wasn't so great. (I told you I wasn't spoiled.)

Every time I turned on the kitchen lights, I'd watch, horrified, as hordes of bugs scattered everywhere. They raced into my drawers, cupboards, and microwave. I would squish them with a paper towel, but they never had any guts (sorry to gross you out, but it's true). I mentioned this challenge to my stepmom on the phone, who said, "You need to sit down."

Shepreneur

I thought that was an odd request. Nevertheless, I sat on one of the two mismatched couches that had been donated by family members, which faced the balcony that overlooked the bingo hall where all the seniors in my building frequented.

My stepmom said, "They're cockroaches."

Instantly, I stood up and said, "No, they're not! You haven't seen them, and you don't know what they are!"

I called the landlord and told him what I was experiencing, and he confirmed what my stepmom had said: indeed, they were cockroaches, which was not a common pest where I lived.

"Unfortunately, we can only spray one floor a day, and they just race up to the next level," he said. "So there's nothing we can do about it. Keep your drains plugged, keep the place clean, and keep your lights on."

Well, I kept the apartment clean, and it didn't matter. I kept the lights on, but they just got used to it and stopped scattering. I could have had a disco ball party with strobe lights, and those cockroaches would have only carried on dancing as if I didn't exist. I was glad my bedroom was at the other end of the apartment but was always afraid they'd eventually make their way over.

(Oh, the nightmares of cockroaches every night!)

I kept working. I moved from the cockroach-infested apartment and eventually moved from Hamilton. I did odds-and-ends jobs like preparing people's taxes, landscaping, and babysitting. I worked as a part-time receptionist at a clinic. Occasionally, I made fake IDs for underage kids. My dad had two cars, and since it was winter, he said, "Why don't you use our extra car for getting to and from work for a couple of weeks while the weather is bad?"

At this point, I was working at a grocery store and popular chicken restaurant. I took him up on his offer. Then I bought tickets to a nightclub for myself and friends to celebrate New Year's Eve, and as I drove too fast to get the tickets, I crashed the vehicle. I fishtailed and went into oncoming traffic and ended up in a ditch.

My dad was not pleased. He picked my friends and me up at the bus station that was en route to the nightclub and took us all home. That was the end of that. I was really on my own.

However, that didn't turn out to be such a bad thing.

To earn more, learn more.

It sounds simple, but it's true. If you want to move up in life, you've got to do what it takes to keep upping your game. To earn more, you must learn more, or business-wise, you'll just have a J.O.B. (just over broke). I appreciate your initiative in taking the time to read this book instead of watching a *desperate housewife* flip over a table (or whatever you're watching) and taking charge of your life.

Learning can be as free as you need it to be. You can learn about nearly anything you need online, or you can listen to podcasts or borrow materials from the library. However, you do it: fill your brain. It's as simple as that. If you're not learning and excelling, then I guarantee someone else in your field is (and you can guess how that's going to turn out for you).

I'm always looking to upgrade myself, so I love to read and listen to motivational and educational podcasts or interviews on YouTube. I listen to podcasts or watch YouTube nearly every morning and evening; it's how I like to start and end my days.

When I'm not watching or listening to something motivational in my morning and evening routine or while at the gym, I watch *America's Funniest Home Videos* or *Just for Laughs: Gags*. If I want a good cry, I'll watch *Britain's Got Talent*'s golden buzzer moments.

I prefer to take in something uplifting for mind, spirit, and business. I have probably four hundred books at my house related to real estate, entrepreneurial pursuits, changing your business, or working less while working smarter.

It's sink or swim, bitches, sink or swim.

I've always had that mentality. People tell me I shouldn't worry about reading on a given night or doing other kinds of work or growth activities.

"What will happen if you don't do that work?" they ask.

I reply, "Someone else will—and they're called my competition."

Now, life isn't a big race, and we do need to stop and smell the roses from time to time, as they say. But I've always been of the mindset that you need to upgrade your knowledge and continually seek to better yourself.

It seems that people only take responsibility for their actions if it got them somewhere good in life. But if their choices created unfavourable experiences, then they blame everyone else for their mishaps. It shouldn't be a pointing-of-fingers game of who messed up or missed an opportunity. Choose to move forward, do the things you should be doing, and forget about the past. You can't change it anyway.

You shouldn't blame anyone else for where you are in life, and not even yourself, because shame isn't good either. Forget about the "mistakes" or "poor decisions" you've made in the past. Put your big girl/boy pants on, and do something about it if you don't like your current situation or in any aspect of your life. Start encouraging yourself and those around you. Life is much easier this way; the world is not out to get you.

One good example of swimming instead of sinking is when I had conditionally bought a triplex, and during the home inspection, it came up that it had asbestos. I got three quotes on the asbestos repair, which surprisingly ranged from $6,000 to $117,000. By this point, I had a lot of experience swimming in the real estate game, so I only showed the homeowner the $117,000 quote, and they agreed to take that off the price.

I bought the property and got the asbestos remedied by the company that charged $6,000. (I'm not saying this to sound deceitful, but you have to be smart about things. The sellers could have gotten their own quotes and done their due diligence, but they did not, and so I made over $100,000 that day.)

Shepreneur

One thousand percent: there are no accidents in excellence.

At my grade 8 graduation, a fellow named Barry LeDuc and I won every award they had. My dad was kneeling at the front, taking photos as they announced the next winner for an award, which happened to be my name. As I walked up to the stage, one of the other parents muttered, "Let someone else win one." It wasn't a matter of chance; I earned what I worked for.

Success comes to those who practice, study their hearts out, research, and put in the muscle. People are fooling themselves if they think it's sheer luck. I call bullshit. Whoever believes excellence is luck is just lazy and doesn't want to put in the effort to succeed. That's their cop-out; it all comes down to hard work.

Sometimes excellence requires creativity.

See, I never talked back to my parents. I had lots of friends who told their parents they hated them, or to fuck off, or that they weren't fair, but I was never a talk-back kid. I did well in school, and I did everything I was told to do. I did all my homework, and I put myself to bed. No one had to say to me, "It's past your bedtime." I guess you could say I was a goody two-shoes. (Okay, yes, you can say it. See grade 8 award ceremony story above.)

On one occasion, I'd forgotten to turn in an assignment that was worth some massive amount of marks. If I didn't deliver it that day by a specific time, I would get a zero. Even though I wasn't yet sixteen and didn't have a driver's license, I ran home and took my stepdad's keys to his vehicle, drove it to my high school, dropped off the assignment, returned his car, and walked back to school. It was a joyride with a purpose, and I could have gotten away with it too (my stepdad was sleeping as he worked nights). Unfortunately, the neighbour saw and tattled on me, and I was grounded anyway.

As an adult, I haven't let up. I'm a very productive person, and I get a lot done at stores at nighttime since both Home Depot and Lowes are open till 10:00 PM. For example, if I have a listing presentation that runs till 9:15 PM, I'll run to Home Depot afterward to get all the stuff I need the next day for my contractors. Then I'll run to Walmart to get all the things I need for my cleaning staff because it's open until 11:00 PM, where I am. (P.S. Walmart gods, please bring back your location open twenty-four hours to Barrie!) Then I'd go home and work or go to the gym.

My overachiever mindset when I was young continues. I still like to have way too much on my plate. It's how I work best. When I was waitressing, if I had one table, I would screw everything up, but if I had eighteen tables, I'd be right on the ball. Everything would be perfect. Everybody would have their drinks, their food, and cutlery. When you give me only one thing to do, my brain goes mushy and doesn't work. I'm good with having more things to do than somebody should have on their plate. Call me weird; I don't care. I'm good with me.

There will always be things that could derail you— some little, some big—but keep trekking through.

I've hit some bumps in the road, that's for damn sure. But that's life; shit happens. If a real estate client betrays you, you can't throw in the towel and say that real estate is a scam and think that you'll never make any money. I can almost guarantee that you're going to have issues on your way to success, no matter your career choice, but you can't give up so easily.

I had a client, and her fiancé was my client, and his parents had been my clients for a decade. After I sold my client's house, she said she wanted to rent for a bit and asked if I knew of a place. The basement apartment I owned (which was also where I lived) was coming available, so she set up a time to view it and decided to take it.

You think you know people, right?

Her fiancé was a contractor I hadn't used before. But I knew his family, and his brother was a good friend of mine from the past. So I hired him to do a gut renovation of a duplex I'd just purchased. I usually buy all the pretty things, such as counters, lights, vanities, and flooring. The contractors buy the "ugly" stuff, such as drywall, screws, pipes, etc. (Poor screws and drywalls—I'm giving them a complex.)

The contractor had just been through a recent separation before meeting my client, so money was a bit tight. Since he couldn't float the ugly side of the job, he asked me to set up a charge account for him at the local building supply store to get what he needed. He wanted a $10,000 deposit, which was relatively common for a $40,000 job, so I agreed.

I visited the site on the second day, and he'd already gutted it, so I approvingly nodded as I went around, impressed with his progress so early in the process. As the weeks passed, he asked for more money in increments of $2,500 or $5,000. I called the building company, and they said he'd spent $6,000 in materials that month, so I thought the work was happening—but stupidly, I didn't check for myself. I let the busyness of other things in my life and business take precedence.

Well, he moved into my basement with my client, and she stopped paying rent, and the two of them lived rent-free on my back for three and a half months. He didn't do any work on the renovation duplex, aside from the initial gutting. When I realized everything he was buying on my tab at the building store wasn't going in my house, I stopped the account.

Next, I gave her notice to pay by a specific date, but instead, she moved out and paid nothing. Then she declared bankruptcy, so the court order I obtained for the back rent wasn't enforceable. I could have gone to the credit agency for relief, but I would have only been able to get 40 percent, and since she wasn't working, then good luck to me in getting blood from that stone.

Let me be the first to tell you that that experience sucked big time. Did I let it stop me? Did I sour on real estate? Did I start thinking all clients would turn into jerks? Nope, nope, and nope: I kept at the real estate game. I wouldn't be here right now if I'd given up.

I bought that home—that he was supposed to renovate—for $140,000 and later sold it for $345,000. As time went on, I got better and better with my buys, so the profit would go higher and higher and have a shorter turn-around window.

When something like that happens to me, I think, "Oh, the universe is really testing me today, yowzers! Well, fuck you, universe, because I got this! You can't throw me off my course or frazzle me! I'll show you. I'm strong! I will conquer this day and this mess of a situation! This is just a speed bump on my road to greatness, so nice try, but sorry for you, that's not going to deter me. Run along now universe. I have bigger fish to fry."

Chapter 2

Determination

Play Full Out

There are two paths to success, and you have to be on both of them at the same time.

> First, you have to work it.
> Second, you have to love it.

Think of waterskiing on one foot—even if you're super skilled, eventually, you're going to wipe out in the water—and believe me, that water feels like a brick wall when you hit. (Once I thought I gave myself an enema while wearing a white bikini. True story. Not fun.)

But if you have both feet down, one on each path, there is a much better chance you will reach your destination.

When I was younger, my dream was to be a plastic surgeon. Of course, that requires a lot of schooling. After moving out and not having parents around bugging me to do homework, I realized I didn't really like homework at all. Forget about medical school. Fortunately, I was self-aware enough to know I needed a new plan.

I was thinking about the full picture of my partner, kids, and so forth, and I didn't want to be thirty years old by the time

Shepreneur

I graduated from university. At that time, I thought thirty was too old to have kids. So I started considering other professions.

I looked at being a lawyer, but I thought they were shady and lied (no offense to any lawyers out there). However, it was the extended years of schooling that was the real turnoff. I considered being a chiropractor, but that would also involve such extended years of education that I might as well have become a plastic surgeon. I thought about being an accountant, but I thought I'd be too bored.

Then my grandma suggested that I become a massage therapist. She used to do visualizations with me all the time when I was young. We'd pretend we were on a plane, and we would visit different clouds where we would receive massages. Or we'd land on a cloud and do some form of meditation and relaxation. So her suggestions made a lot of sense to me, considering our history.

My dad was always around other surgeons and liked to brag about me when I was in high school. He would say to them, "My daughter's in the top two percent in Ontario," or "My daughter won this award," or "My daughter is this, and my daughter is that." I thought that my dad would be disappointed if I went to massage therapy school because then he wouldn't necessarily have anything to brag about. It was the story I had in my head that I would disappoint him, but my dad said he loved me and only wanted my happiness.

I called the massage school the next day and learned that I could take classes for eighteen months with no summer or March break or go for two years with a pause. It sounded perfect, and I would be out of school at just nineteen years of age. Easy breezy.

So I started massage school, which changed my life. It wasn't becoming a massage therapist that changed my life but meeting a friend in massage school who lived an hour north of the city.

One day, she casually informed me that her mortgage cost less than my rent. I had no idea if houses cost $5,000, $50,000, $500,000 or $5 million. Real estate and the price of houses weren't on my radar at all when I was nineteen. I asked how much houses cost, and she told me an approximation at the time. She explained that I would need a down payment, and when I asked how much down payments were, she said they were usually 5 percent of the total cost of the house.

Thinking about all the money I'd saved by working three jobs, if homes were really as cheap as she said they were, I figured why waste money on rent?

Do not—I repeat—do not do something just for the money.

I know that in the previous chapter, I said that no job is beneath you—and it isn't. The key is to use your employment to strategically climb the ladder of success. Just because you start at the bottom doesn't mean you have to stay there.

However, there's a bigger piece to this puzzle (isn't there, always?):

You need to love what you do.

Shepreneur

You have to figure out what you love because that makes all the difference. Let me be clear about why: if you're passionate, you'll be determined enough to play full out.

My parents met and married during their first year at university. They were having problems and thought that a child would bring them together, and that didn't quite work out. Lots of people over the years have asked me if I hoped they'd get back together, and "Absolutely not!" would always be my answer.

They split up when I was two years old, and I could never picture them together back then or let alone ever again. I was not one of those kids who went off to university and then got the call that my parents were bored, or they've grown in different directions, or it's just not working.

I don't remember them being together at all.

My dad remarried when I was five years old, and I decided (unconsciously at that time, remaining unaware of it for another three decades) that I was alone, and I had to do everything on my own. This mindset helped me because it made me very motivated, driven, and successful.

My parents didn't want me to be spoiled. Even though I had four stepsiblings, none of them lived in the same house as me, so I grew up as an only child. My dad didn't want me to be a spoiled only child, let alone a spoiled surgeon's daughter, so he mentored me and showed me the value of working hard and saving money. I paid attention.

Kristin Cripps

When I was a tween, my dad was receiving a lot of job offers in the states. I went with him and my stepmom to check out the clinics and the schools and dance academies in these various locations. Chattanooga, Tennessee, came up as the winner, and they were seriously contemplating the move. My stepbrothers were older with lives, jobs, and girlfriends of their own, but since I was young and still at home, I was part of the decision to move.

Even though I was too young to be privy to actual numbers, I remember my stepmom asking my dad, "If it wasn't for the money, would we still go to Chattanooga?"

My dad said, "Absolutely not." They looked at each other until my dad said, "Well, we have our answer." And that was that— we stayed in Canada.

Their conversation was one of those pivotal moments that stuck with me. My dad and stepmom were in a position to make decisions based on what fueled their passion rather than what brought in the most money. They loved doing what they did in Canada, so there we remained.

When you're going after your goals, make sure it's the joy and excitement and passion you're pursuing. Because if it's just the money, it won't work out. Sorry to burst your bubble, but an empty journey won't lead to a full life. To reach financial independence and live a life you love, you must have all that other good stuff driving you too.

Shepreneur

To think that everything is going to be ideal and perfect is not reality.

Depending on your age, you might remember the "shit happens" fad.

That it does, and do not dwell on it! Do not make a story about it. If you do, that story will live in your head and come with you into your future, and your decisions will be influenced by it. For example, "I can't trust people," or "People always let me down." If you tell yourself stories like these, they will prohibit you from living in the now.

Life is not all roses and daffodils. Shit acts as a fertilizer to make those flowers grow, so if you don't have some shit in your life, then how do you expect the beauty to grow and evolve into something bigger and more beautiful?

Nothing comes easy. Everything is hard work. Whether it's getting that better body, making that massive paycheque, having that awkward conversation, not taking the easy way out, or having that stable relationship, you're going to have to put some muscle into it.

If you think everything should be perfect and there are never going to be any hardships, then you are going to have rude awakenings way more times than you'll want to count. Be prepared. Know it's all a part of the ride. See what you can learn from it, and keep trudging forward.

I didn't jump from massage school into real estate and become a millionaire overnight. Probably like most folks, my path was rocky and full of detours and sharp lefts and rights.

For about six years or so, I was the "ring girl" whenever there was a fundraiser for police against firefighters in an American Gladiator type of joust. I wore tiny outfits that I bought from stripper websites or lingerie that I cut and mixed and matched to make out of the ordinary shocking outfits as I did with most of my bartending outfits.

This was back in the day when people used cameras and not cell phones, and when my dad looked at my digital camera one day while I was on a walk with my stepmom, he saw these photos. I knew I'd let him down when we returned from our walk, and he asked, "What the hell are you doing?" He had the camera in hand, pointing at the photos.

Um, making money?

He didn't know where or why my pictures were taken; he just saw me in the outfits. He is not one for skimpy outfits and would prefer me in a suit or something classy and respectable. Perhaps he thought I was going to be a prostitute, a stripper, or something of the sort?

Anyway, while attending massage school, I was living with a roommate who was obsessed with getting naked wherever we went and was hell-bent on becoming a stripper. We went to different strip clubs all the time, and she would take notes of what she did and didn't like. There's an area in Toronto known for the crossroads of Jane and Finch. Our massage school was on Finch, and there was a strip club nearby we would often visit.

Shepreneur

My roommate worked out an approximation of how much we could earn per night as strippers and how much money we could bank and save. We spoke to the owner one night (who had some weird nickname like Rooster or Chicken), and he said we could start that same weekend. I was still a virgin, so can you imagine a virgin stripper? Everyone assumed I was the opposite, of course.

I had a boyfriend at the time, and we went to see a movie called *Serendipity*. The main character wrote her number on the inside of a book and then sold the book to a secondhand bookstore. She felt that if they were meant to meet again, he'd find the book, and that would mean it was destiny.

For the record, the kind of movie where people leave and say, "Oh my God, that was so predictable! What an awful chick flick!" will practically guarantee that I'll leave the theatre bawling my eyes out and thinking it was the best movie ever made. So I bawled my eyes out at the theatre and told my boyfriend what myself and my roommate had planned and said I didn't want to do it. Stripping felt like the opposite of serendipity and romance.

This same roommate wanted to save more and make more money by sharing a room with me (not just the apartment) and grow some things in her bedroom (um, ya, not happening). She wasn't exactly full of great ideas.

One day, I came home to find her sitting on the couch and petting a raccoon while feeding it. It was her chore to take out the garbage, and I didn't know she hadn't been doing so and was instead throwing it onto the balcony, which was right off her bedroom. The garbage had accumulated, creating a haven for wild animals. Why not coerce the raccoon inside since it was so cute and all?

And some people wonder why I choose to live alone.

So we didn't start stripping (I was definitely questioning her influence on me), and instead, I started bartending and moved out on my own.

I was always looking for a way to hustle the hardest or be the most effective at the nightclub game. While bartending, I moved around from club to club until I eventually settled where I brought home the most money in one shift. I was also continually running social experiments to see what behaviours netted me more money.

I'd test if I made better tips if I first spoke to the guy or the girl. I would test different outfits that I made from lingerie and stripper outfits and enhancing them with "chicken cutlets" (as I called the padded inserts made of jelly you could add to round out your bra).

I learned that I would sell a similar amount of booze, but I would make double and triple my tips when I wore smaller outfits with chicken cutlets. Other bartenders would question my skimpy clothing, but I always replied, "Hey, I still have my clothes on, and they're larger than a bathing suit. Plus, I have this bar to protect me from customers. They can't touch me, so what do I care?"

Shepreneur

At one nightclub where I worked, there was a bed upstairs. Why a bed? So the married owner with two children could sleep with girls he desired and chose during the evenings. Was this an ideal situation for me to be in? Absolutely not. But I had bills to pay, so I was kind of like a horse with blinders on; I didn't look at the stuff going around me and just focused on my hustle and the tips.

Whether you're trying to be a successful realtor or investor, lose fifty pounds, or develop a thriving relationship, it's all about what you put into it. Take action to achieve those successes and leave everything that won't work or will get in your way on the wayside.

Persist until you succeed, and then keep growing and adding to what you have conquered, so you don't flatline. I get that it's easier just to keep doing the same things, but we only enjoy one time around on this planet, so why not make it a stunner and rock it like nobody's business?!

Always challenge yourself to go bigger, better, higher, faster.

I mentioned earlier that I worked three jobs at a time after I finished massage school. I always had extra money because of my bartending gig and a full-time day job massaging. For years, I would massage every day from 9:00 AM to 4:00 PM, then waitress from 5:00 to 10:00 PM at a fine dining steakhouse. Then I would bartend from 11:00 to 3:00 or 3:30 AM back in Toronto.

Then I'd wake up and do it all again.

Kristin Cripps

Two days of this schedule paid my bills for the month, and I usually worked every single day, never taking a day off. The money quickly accumulated, as you can imagine. And although I was always interested in homes and real estate, friends or the people I was dating would say, "You already have three jobs! Having a rental would be like having a fourth job, so don't do it."

Stupidly, I listened for a while, but eventually, I got smart, decided to stop listening, and buy duplexes.

At twenty-one, I decided I wanted to sell my house and take half of the money I made and travel around the world for three years, then use the other half to buy a new home when I got back. I told my parents while serving them at the restaurant where I worked, and they said they thought it was a great idea. I thought it was odd and went to the kitchen to get another customer's food and came back to the table, and they said, "Or you can stay here, get married, and have us some babies."

There it was: their truth came out.

I liked the contrast in working my three jobs: the change from my quiet, peaceful massage days with all my clients sleeping to serving at the steak house to the fast-paced, busy nightclub world. I liked bartending because I got to be out, dance, and listen to music while doing shots, not to mention having fun with outfits and leaving with a wad of cash.

After my bartending shifts, we would all go upstairs, and I'd whip my cutlets out and throw them on the table because they were heavy and would give me a headache. Then we'd count our money.

Shepreneur

There is a line from "Work It," a Missy Elliott song that I liked, about how ladies shouldn't feel shame but make sure they were ahead of the game. I'd be like, "Yep, yep," as I swiped my customers' money into my overflowing tip bucket. "I'm ahead of it. People, give me your tips."

So fast-forward to buying a home. It was not my first one, but one I bought when I was not yet licensed and didn't yet know the rules under the money-laundering and terrorist act. I was at my realtor's home doing up the offer after an afternoon of showings, and she asked, "How much do you want to put down as a deposit?"

I said, "I'm not sure. Hang on a minute." I came back with my shirt hem pulled up to my chin, flipped it down, dumped a pile of cash on the table, and started counting. She looked at me as if I was a drug dealer, but cash was the world I knew, and it didn't seem odd to me. I used to keep money in my glove box until it was overflowing, then I'd haul it to the bank. (Sorry, hijackers, if you want to take my vehicle today, all you're going to find in there now are some random spoons, a jar of Nutella, and maybe a few tampons and toothpicks.)

What's the point in sharing my crazy, sleepless early years? To back up my advice that you always challenge yourself. Sure, I missed out on a lot of sleep during those years, but it paid off—handsomely.

Be relentless in the pursuit of whatever sets your soul on fire (yes, yes!).

When I was twenty-three, I was rear-ended and needed to go through my insurance to get my car fixed. The insurer covered a certain amount per day to go toward a car rental. I had my eye on a sports car, so I asked if I could pay the difference to get the sports car instead while they repaired my vehicle. I called around and found a company that rented high-end rides. I told them which one I wanted, and they told me the price.

They had a driver pick me up and take me to their showroom. He looked at my driver's license and saw that I was twenty-three years old and said, "You have to be over twenty-five years old to rent this car."

After arguing back and forth (my negotiation skills weren't very developed at that time), I was driven back home. I then took my junky rental to the new car dealership that had that same car I wasn't allowed to rent. The dealership management wouldn't even let me test-drive it.

Frustrated, I drove for thirty minutes to another dealership, and they let me test-drive one of the two on the lot—they had a silver one and a royal blue one—and I picked the silver one which was stick shift. I'd never driven a stick in my life, and you could tell. However, out of sheer stubbornness, I bought the car that day: a brand-new Nissan 350Z convertible, in the first year it was manufactured.

At the same time, I was conditionally sold on a duplex and had been planning to put $65,000 down that I'd saved from bartending. I'd just had the home inspection done that day. Stupidly, I put the money toward the car instead and backed out during the home inspection (and that house went up tremendously in value). But I had a messy hairdo and pile of speeding tickets to make up for it.

Shepreneur

I was mad that they wouldn't let me rent the car due to my age, then I was mad that I couldn't test-drive it. Looking back, it wasn't a smart move to just go buy the damn thing, but it was my "Summer of Fun" car, as I called it.

Not even a week after buying the car, I went to the nightclub where I worked, and the manager was standing outside, rocking his signature hairdo, a long braid down to his butt (it's still hanging there today). He grabbed my hand and pulled me backward as I went inside to grab my till and set up my bar. He asked, "Who did *you* marry?" and nodded his head at the car.

That's something that would never cross my mind. Why would someone think I had a nice car only because someone gave it to me and not because I worked my ass off and slept an average of three hours a night seven days a week for years?

I had a best friend who came from a very well-off family (including a lot of NHL players and businesspeople), and he professed his love for me during my Summer of Fun. I would never have thought of dating him, let alone marrying him; I thought of him as a brother and a best friend. So it was just weird for me.

I had friends that I never thought would pick someone for money who were urging me to marry him, "You'll be set for life, and even if you divorce him in a few months, who cares? It will be worth it." I could never fathom pretending I loved someone just to be "set for life."

No, thanks!

Financial independence means that you don't have to work if you don't want to; you have enough money to live well and comfortably until you're a hundred years old.

Once you've reached a certain income, the money portion of the game becomes less important. I was on strict budgets when I was younger when doing renovations, and I would have to know to the penny what I was spending. If we needed five more tiles on a job, sometimes I'd have to say no, because I even counted waste. Now, if a contractor asks for a certain amount, I will agree to move forward if it makes sense.

I don't care as much about the money these days. I'm no longer holding my breath every time my visa is swiped at the grocery store and peeking through one eyelid to see if it says "declined" or "approved" like I used to do. I'm able to create without having to be so cost conscious. Now I'm not saying I'll pay a stupid amount of money for something when I can get a less-expensive version, but some things do not have knockoff versions, so I must and can pay top price.

Being financially independent means you don't have to budget or think about how much you spend. You can do the things you want to do, whether you get paid for it or not. I don't discuss numbers with anyone besides my accountant, my parents, and, occasionally, this one friend. The only reason I talk about finances with this particular friend is that we are on par with each other.

Shepreneur

This particular friend and I know that neither person is out to get the other, so we can talk easily about our financial status. In general, it can be challenging to have conversations about money if you're not on par. Some people will ask for loans that they don't intend on paying back or want freebies. I've found that they will often take advantage of situations, so I like to leave conversations around money out of it. I lost a seventeen-year friendship over this kind of stuff.

I know the general advice we hear is to have friends in better positions than you emotionally, financially, and spiritually, but I'd say we're pretty evenly matched. A couple of years ago, we made a tally of all the properties we had, what we owed on them, what they were worth at the time, and how much equity we had, and then added them up.

I had never tallied my properties before that and have not done it since. My friend said something along the lines of "Crippsy, it's time to see how rich we are!" and he laughed. I realized that I was financially independent at that local Irish pub over a cider and nachos.

I'm not a flaunty person and have never been. Until I launched a recent online course, people didn't know if I made $5, $50,000, $500,000, or $50 million a year. I acted the same as everyone else. When this friend and I tallied our properties, it was the first time I knew I had multimillions. I knew I had a lot of equity and could guesstimate what I had but had never done the precise number crunching before.

It was kind of a "holy shit" moment that day at the pub when he and I both realized what we had created for ourselves.

So how did I go from massage therapist to fine dining server to bartender to real estate mogul?

Read on!

Chapter 3

Business

Where There's a Will, There's a Way

Owning a business is hard work.

When I was three years old, I was given a little doll in a carrying pouch as a gift. I took the doll out and filled the bag with marbles instead. I wanted to wear it on my back like a backpack; however, since there was no zipper or Velcro, every time I tried to slip one arm through the strap, and then the other, all the marbles would fall out. I worked diligently for over three hours (my dad confirmed this) until, eventually, I succeeded in getting it onto my back without any of the marbles falling out.

It's the same with running a business. There will be times when you have to focus on the little things and work hard and persevere until you reach your goal—even if it's something simple like getting marbles on your back.

I read that Oprah said that the only difference between billionaires and millionaires is that billionaires say no more often. When you have money, you're always going to have people asking for help or investment in projects they have going on. The cool thing is that you get to decide what you want to do with your money. You can give it all away or invest it or keep it all for yourself. There's no judgment. It's your money.

Shepreneur

Author Rafael Badziag interviewed self-made billionaires for his Amazon best-seller, *The Billion Dollar Secret: 20 Principles of Billionaire Wealth and Success*. He found the difference between millionaires and billionaires came down to one question: do you enjoy making it or spending it more?

Badziag found that billionaires enjoy making it more and millionaires enjoy spending it more. I guess I'll never be a billionaire (I might have a "bit" of a shopping problem), but I'm okay with that. I'd rather have the ride of a lifetime than not enjoy my time here. Some people might not consider working three jobs and sleeping three hours a night "enjoying it," but hey, that wasn't forever, and it paid off in the long term!

So how did I get my start?

Let's jump in.

When the friend from massage school told me that her mortgage was less than my rent, I was intrigued and curious to see what I could own for less than I was paying to my landlord. By nineteen, I had a bit over $80,000 saved from bartending, which was way more than the 5 percent down payment I needed for my $143,000 home. Before my dad knew how much money I'd socked away, he offered to match my deposit but quickly retracted that when he found out how much I had saved serving drunk people at the bar.

I went out with a realtor my parents had found and saw three or four townhomes in Barrie and said, "I'll come back next weekend and look at more." When he told me they were all pretty much the same, I picked one and proceeded to buy and close on my first house. It was a middle-unit townhouse with three bedrooms, three bathrooms, and an unfinished walkout basement.

I finished the basement myself, which I should not have done—a classic rookie mistake. The walls were wonky, and things were not level. But I was a save-money, do-it-yourself person when I should have been at the bar making money. I should have paid somebody else to do the job and not tried to skimp corners because it did not look good when I finished. Let's be honest.

So lesson learned.

But I was going to have many more lessons to learn.

My first purchase was such a quick pick, and there was no thought put into it. When I moved in, I started noticing that, structurally and layout-wise, the townhouse didn't work. I would say to myself, "It would be better if this wall were over there or that door was over here."

There were no side windows, as the home wasn't an end unit. I couldn't add a window for natural light on the side, so the place was dark. Tons of times since then, I've added new windows to homes, installed larger windows, or put in sliding doors. But I couldn't do anything to that unit because there were other people attached to either side.

I didn't do a lot of renovations in that property besides finishing the basement and painting. My plan was for massage clients to come to my house for sessions, and that wouldn't work there. Plus, the guys next door had parties all the time. The people to the left of me had their whole backyard filled with sunflowers. It just wasn't the greatest neighbourhood for me or to have a home massage business.

My boyfriend at the time and his mother were upset by my purchase, as they were traditional Italians and had our whole lives planned out for us. We were to get married, then live with them for five years while we saved to buy a house on their street. Then we would be expected to have children and live happily ever after.

They couldn't understand why I would buy a house without him, let alone have it an hour away from their family. And God forbid they would have to tell the grandma what Kristin had done! A regular at the sports bar where I worked was so happy to learn that I had bought a house that he bought a round of drinks for everyone at the bar to celebrate. (I later ended up dating and living with him, but that's another story.)

At my age, all my friends were talking about going on fun trips, but I had to make sure I had enough money to pay my mortgage. I had to consider that if I went on a trip, I wouldn't make tips or wages for the week I was gone, plus I would still have bills and the cost of the vacation, so it was kind of like a triple whammy I had to consider. I had already been used to paying bills for five years, so I was pretty accustomed to the financial scenario.

My stepmom had told me that if you can pay for everything you need to for the month with one weeks' pay, then you're good. If you need three weeks to make your car payment, rent or mortgage, utilities, and groceries, then you'll be in trouble when things go sideways, as they often do. I used her excellent advice as a general guideline for years.

The thing that surprised me about my first home purchase was that shitty neighbours could make you decide to move. Three single guys lived to the right of me, and they each had their kids every other weekend. So when the kids were over, they were excellent.

But the rest of the time, it was like living next to the busiest resort at spring break—everyone was partying and passing out on the lawn and front steps. Not fun. Plus, I could hear everything through the walls, which, believe me, *really* wasn't much fun.

Then—and I'm not going to lie—I was offended when my dad said that my townhouse was a great *starter* house. While I know he didn't mean anything offensive by it, I was upset. I thought, "I'm going to live here forever, I'm going to have my kids here, and my grandkids here, and I am never going to move!"

Four months later—cue noisy frat house next door—I put the home up for sale.

Remember when I said that everyone is a millionaire? Here are some comments from the typical "excuse" millionaires I hear *all the time*:

- ❑ "Well, if I was your age, I could become a landlord."
- ❑ "If I was a contractor or handy, I could do it."
- ❑ "I work too much as it is to be a landlord."
- ❑ "I'm too busy with the kids."

- ☐ "I don't know enough about real estate."
- ☐ "What if the tenants don't pay?"
- ☐ "I don't have deep enough pockets in case something terrible happens."

You don't have to be a Harvard graduate to make money in real estate. Regular people make money in real estate all the time. Some may think that you can only invest if you were born into oil money, related to a movie star, won the lottery, received an inheritance, or won $5 million in a settlement. But you don't need to check any of those boxes to make money in real estate.

Anyway, I didn't know all that when I was nineteen. I had to learn for myself. I heard so many absurd stories that I quickly sold my first home and moved to a brand new build in a better area, which brings me to my second point.

Don't take advice about the stock market from someone who has never had stock or invested in one.

I'm not referring only to the stock market either. You shouldn't take advice from anyone who isn't a leader in their industry or did it themselves in some shape or form with success. For example, let's say you want to learn how to become a real estate success.

Realtors always joke that if you get pulled over and asked for your driver's license, you're more likely to have a real estate license than a driver's license. So many people have a real estate license, but most of them are making less than minimum wage. To learn how to make money in real estate, you need to find a realtor who's in the top 1 percent in sales and ask them to mentor you.

The people at the top search for answers and do what few actually do. Look up those people currently doing it and ask for their guidance in the market. What insight can they provide for you? How can you take that great advice for your market, apply it, then copy and duplicate it over and over?

You don't want to pick a realtor who sells less than 8 or 10 houses a year. You want a realtor selling 40, 50, 60, 100, or 150 homes a year because they'll have the insider knowledge and experience that other realtors don't. If you get in with the top earners, then they can help you grow a massive portfolio.

If they are investors too, then even better because they've been in the mud and have the firsthand knowledge you're seeking. But if you can't find that kind of mentor, you can always watch shows on YouTube and read up on different investing options. (But keep in mind that everybody has their method and works differently.)

I believe it's always good to seek advice from people who are in a better position than you are on a subject. Refusing to take advice on the stock market from someone who has never had a stock or invested in one seems like common sense to me, but believe me, it's not.

How do I know this

Because for too long, I listened to other people.

Shepreneur

Remember the first townhouse I bought? I wanted to keep it, so I asked others' opinions if they thought I should keep it and use it as a rental.

My dad and stepmom told me a good thirty or so horror stories about why I should not become a landlord. There would be people living in the house who wouldn't pay for months and maybe even years, and I'd have to get giant biker dudes to remove them forcibly. Or I'd have to light the house on fire to smoke them out. Ludicrous stories, now that I think back.

I'm sure things were different because they were telling me stories from the seventies, but being a young kid, I idolized my dad and thought he knew everything in the world. So I sold it.

Then, when the townhome sold a year and a half later, those next owners made a boatload of money. I sent the listing to my dad, and he asked, "Why didn't you keep that townhome as a rental?"

From then on, I made the decision not to listen to people. But even though I said so, I still listened to people. I'd think about buying a place and hear, "You have three jobs, and you have enough on your plate."

Then I'd watch the prices go up and up and up on the house I didn't buy.

I watched as others bought homes at $150,000 and would sell them for $310,000 two years later. The market kept going up and up, and they were all the houses that I wanted to make an offer on, and I listened to somebody else and didn't pull the trigger.

I finally decided to do whatever I felt was right for me. If I lost money, then it would be on me, and so be it. I made up my mind to do my own thing instead of listening to the opinions of others.

Insert superwoman with a cape.

Be okay with the fact that most times, your path won't be straight.

That first townhouse piqued my interest in real estate. Since I made more money than my mortgage and utilities just doing massage, and I was waitressing and bartending, I had a lot of cash. I started to look at other avenues to make money, such as buying additional properties. Because I love decorating the inside, knocking walls down, and furnishing it afterward, purchasing and renovating real estate was a no-brainer for me.

Next, I bought a bungalow, and I should have kept that one (but I was listening to other people back then). It's on one of the most popular streets in Barrie, besides the waterfront, and if I still owned that house, I would have an extra $500,000 in equity.

(I told you it took me a few tries before I had the real estate game down pat.)

When I told my dad that I had failed my first massage therapy practical, he was supportive. My stepmom shared that she'd failed her first dental hygiene exam, and that was helpful to hear. My dad shared that in his first semester at university, he averaged a thirty-two due to partying too hard and was able to turn it around. (I'm pretty sure he averaged ninety-eight in med school and was the valedictorian, so he put in the hours and determination to achieve his goals.)

During my first day working at a spa, I'd been booked appointments every hour on the hour for ten or eleven hours straight. No one told me that you're supposed to short all your clients by a few minutes to give them time to change, so you can clean up the room and get ready for the next client. Consequently, by the end of the day, I was exhausted, hadn't eaten anything all day or gone to the bathroom, and was ridiculously behind schedule.

Eventually, I got the idea to open a spa. I imagined driving my convertible to the spa from wherever I was shopping, checking on the place, and my employees would tell me that everything was going swimmingly as the dollar signs *cha-chinged* in my head. The casino noises went off in the background, and I drove off, laughing with my friends as I returned to my fabulous life.

Consequently, the third time I almost became a stripper was when I opened that spa. Bartending had previously saved me from learning the tricks of the pole and that hustle. (I used to refer to bartending as "stripper money without taking your clothes off.") But when I opened my spa, I thought it was time to grow up, so I quit bartending and serving cold turkey. I thought I should own a spa, massage people, have staff, advertise, and be a grown-up.

I had no idea how to make money at that venture, even though I had worked at a spa since I was nineteen years old. My spa was called Elysium, which means heavenly or blissful in Greek, but my spa was no heaven for me as I was losing money like nobody's business.

My staff spilled hundreds of dollars of products and shrugged their shoulders and said, "Oopsie!" One girl dropped a one-thousand-dollar jug of serum on the floor and didn't bat an eyelash. They would subtract tax instead of adding it. They would not show up for work. They'd go out with me after work and expect me to pay for everything.

One girl backed into a client's car when leaving and then panicked and hit it again and squealed off, only to call me later to tell me what happened. Then the price of advertising killed me since I paid so much out and took so little in.

When I figured out that I was going in the hole to the tune of over $15,000 a month, I knew I could not keep up that pace. I again calculated how much I thought I could make stripping, went to a few clubs, but I couldn't do it and fell back into bartending.

(Insert my father saying, "Thank God!")

I have two stepbrothers, and I always wondered what I would do if they came in—I would have been so mortified! In the movie *Coyote Ugly*, there was a scene where the girl was on the bar having a water fight, and her father walked in and almost had a heart attack. He was so ashamed of his little girl and what she was doing for money—and that would have been my dad!

I enjoyed Elysium on some level, but running a spa wasn't what I had anticipated it to be, and I couldn't justify the amount of money I was losing. I closed my spa and went back to the resort where I used to massage. I thought that since schooling had cost so much, I had to continue doing massage for a living, or it would be a waste of time and moola.

But I was sacrificing my spirit and compromising who I was by not doing something that I enjoyed. I didn't enjoy doing massage, and I never had. All I wanted was that dream of showing up in my convertible and driving off and going shopping—never actually working at the spa.

Remember, in the last chapter, how I said you should never do it for the money? Well, I took my advice and decided to shake things up.

Some people had told me that they thought I would do well in real estate sales, but I'd heard a story about a sexual assault taking place at an open house, so I said to myself, "Oh, hell no, I'm not getting raped."

(Insert concrete wall going up around me—locked).

Additionally, there was a realtor friend of the family who had done some inappropriate things to me when I was younger (more on him later), and I associated all realtors with him. So in my head, I was thinking, "Nope, not getting raped and not becoming a slimy realtor."

But as I was buying and selling real estate, I thought I should get a license for my purposes to save 5 percent, which was the norm in my market at that time. But I never planned to do it for a living. I was still looking into other professions or courses

I could take so I could get out of the massage world, but I hadn't decided on anything specific yet.

Everyone discouraged me from becoming a landlord, as I mentioned, but looking back, not one of them was a landlord. It was ridiculous to ask their opinion in the first place. There is the occasional anomaly, but I think the majority of twenty-something-year-olds don't go to seminars or listen to podcasts, have mentors or coaches, and tend to ask people immediately around them. So I asked my family, my friends, and whomever I was dating at the time for real estate advice.

I should have listened to myself and sought out specialists or investors for advice.

Buy property as soon as you can.

Real estate investing gives you a fantastic vessel to do whatever you want, and we know money can't buy happiness, but it sure can buy a lot of things and make life easier. You can give it all away; you can spoil, teach, live out your wildest dreams. Real estate is such an easy way to get passive cash flow so you can live out your true desires.

Who doesn't want to live out their wildest dreams?

The fearful, that's who. I am not one of those thinkers, and neither are you.

Barrie, where I bought my first home, had the third-highest rent in Canada but is now sixth, with Vancouver being first and Toronto second. The average one-bedroom apartment in Barrie is $1,408. And it's likely not some lovely house but could easily be a basement with claustrophobic windows, people banging around upstairs, no control over the heat or air (if there is any), coin laundry, and one parking spot.

Let's say someone lives in a basement apartment during the age of twenty to thirty. Most people won't remain in the basement; they'll move to the main floor and spend $1,700 to $2,000 a month plus utilities. But let's say they live there for ten years. That's $15,600 a year or $156,000 for ten years, assuming they never moved to the main floor, which 98 percent of people do. The sooner someone can get into homeownership, the sooner they can be putting that money toward their mortgage instead of someone else's—a real no brainer for me.

I think that's why I was so adamant about advising my little sister to buy a house when she was to receive around $130,000 on her eighteenth birthday. I'd been talking to her for years about what she was going to do with her inheritance. I'd show her different scenarios on napkins or the back of menus when we went out to dinner. My scribbles always had the same outcome: she was to buy a house upon receiving her inheritance.

She had already made the mistake of telling her boyfriend and friends about her inheritance, and it turned into a free-for-all as they planned an extravagant vacation at her expense. I said to her, "Let's say you buy a $60,000 vehicle, go on a trip, take your friends, and spend $20,000."

Say she went on a shopping spree and spent $5,000, put $30,000 in her bank account and $10,000 in a savings of some sort, and spent $5,000 on tattoos or drinking it away at night clubs. In five years, she would probably still have the $10,000 in savings but will have blown the $30,000, own a car worth perhaps $8,000, have some pictures of a trip, some out-of-style clothing that might not fit, a minuscule amount of money in the bank, a couple of tattoos, and hazy memories of drunken nights and good times.

Or she could buy a house!

Hello! Ding! Ding! Ding!

Had she bought a house at eighteen, she would have paid down her principal over the next five years, enjoyed an escalation in value, and she'd have her original amount plus any equity the house had made. She would have had no shame about poor money decisions with the inheritance of a lifetime that not many eighteen-year-olds have the opportunity to receive.

I wasn't right on her back on her eighteenth birthday, which was a mistake. From the end of May (when she turned eighteen) to the middle of August, she spent over $30,000 taxiing her friends around to different nightclubs and buying alcohol, cigarettes, and clothes for them—she was busy being a rock star that summer.

When I found out about this, I said, "That's it—you're buying a house this week!"

We looked at some places, and she remarked that the townhouses were awful. She claimed to see bullet holes in the windows, but there were no bullet holes. They were great starter houses (oh no, I sound like my dad!), but she wanted the

Shepreneur

Taj Mahal. She said she was not raising her baby in some crack house neighbourhood, as she was pregnant by that time.

So we upped her budget, and we were able to get her into an all-brick detached bungalow with a fully legal basement apartment, a main floor gorgeous kitchen with granite and voila! No more money wasting and a secure foot in the door for her and her son's future.

Barter like a boss.

I barter because I love it, and I don't pretend I don't. I've dated people who are embarrassed by my bartering prowess, but that's their problem. I thrive in barter situations. Perhaps it's a power thing, as I feel like I won if I got it for way under the asking price, or I negotiated a killer deal.

Speaking of bartering, two little boys who looked to be about nine years old knocked at my door and offered to rake my grass for five bucks. I love a hustle mindset starting young and seeing kids working for their extra money instead of just expecting mom and dad to shell it out.

Teenagers could get jobs at the age of fourteen and not wait until they're sixteen, but they're already at the age when "it's not cool to work at that place" or "I don't want my crush coming in and seeing me wearing a hairnet" or whatever their excuse is.

If kids learn at a young age the value of hard work and sales (as they can get turned down at the door), it benefits them so much as teenagers and in their adult lives.

I loved those two little guys, and of course, I gave them more than five dollars. Be a go-getter; don't be lazy! If you are lazy, then don't blame anyone else for your laziness. Sorry not sorry to be the bearer of bad news, but it's all on you.

I went to Egypt with my cousin, who is one year older than me. We found a market and decided to meet back at a certain point at a set time. I returned with an ear-to-ear smile, loaded down with necklaces and scarves and assortments of goodies all under two dollars.

She came back upset and crying and said, "I bought this ugly bracelet, and I don't even like it!" Then she told me that she had paid over $120 for this "silver" bracelet. I had her take me to the vendor, where she bought it to demand her money back. I said, "Shame on you for taking advantage of her!"

I thrive in markets and places where you need to barter because it's a game where I excel. If you haven't yet cultivated this skill, I recommend that you do so.

Fake it till ya make it.

This is a clever tip for solving the catch 22 of needing business experience to get hired, but no one wants to hire you until you have experience. Sometimes you need experience just to apply, but if you don't have any, who will hire you? So I always pretended I had prior experience.

When I was a teenager, I wanted a serving job at a sports bar for some extra money. I liked the idea of having an hourly wage plus tips. I liked knowing I could hustle and work more and get

Shepreneur

paid more—as opposed to no matter how much I worked, I would receive the same amount of money.

When I applied to the sports bar, I chose a place that I knew had closed and said I had worked there, so there was no reference to check. Then I called every two days asking to speak to the manager to see if he had reviewed my resume yet. He told me that he hadn't, and it turned out that someone had thrown it out. But since he liked my persistence, and there was a server there who was slacking off and always late for her shift, he hired me and gave all her shifts to me.

As I said, I didn't plan to become a realtor for profit but only to save the 5 percent I was paying for selling my properties. I started studying for my real estate license at the age of twenty-six. However, I didn't want people to know I was new in the business, so I lied and said I had been in business for six years. But then when I was in it for two years, I couldn't say two, so I said I'd been selling real estate for eight years—and just kept tacking on the years.

I also carried mace in my bra (instead of chicken cutlets) for the first three years, so in case there was ever a dicey or questionable situation, I was prepared. My dad liked that, as he was always worried about his little girl out in the big world.

I wouldn't say I had the biggest supporters at the beginning of my career. I was in a program through the brokerage where I worked. We met once a week and were given things to do between that week and the next.

Everyone encouraged me, such as my family and friends, but they didn't realize that everyone and their brother knows a realtor. My support group expected me to be slammed and busy and successful from the get-go. But it was hard work, and I didn't make money for a long time. I was still bartending and massaging, so that paid the bills while I built my real estate business.

Always push yourself, and be sure to play.

What drives me now is being unstoppable. I don't like to feel stagnant. I think you can only be stagnant for so long before you start to slip backward, and that's not where I want to be. It's like a high because I feel a rush when I get to the next level of something and feel that accomplishment.

I love thinking of something I want to do that may be far-fetched. I enjoy putting the steps in place even if they're small and take an extended amount of time and achieving that higher accomplishment.

Do you think I can't do that?! Watch me!

It also drives me bonkers to sit still. Don't get me wrong, because I love to be still if I'm getting a massage or reading a book. But to relax and not soak in the goodness of a talk or a friend's company or a comedy show doesn't make sense to me. My friends always laugh at me for watching comedy skits, and my ludicrous fully belly bursts of laughter, but that doesn't bother me because I think they're funny. If you don't think so, then be a bump on a log somewhere else—my space is a happy zone.

Shepreneur

I also want to test my limits. I'm sure people who have set world records wish to do the same, but just physically. However, I bet there's a lot of mental clarity and concentration that goes into it too—who are we kidding? An athlete might wonder, "Could I do it .8 seconds faster? Is that humanly possible?"

They train, get coaching, and condition themselves to give it their best shot. I feel the same way. To reach my goals, I train, get coached, and condition myself and try. If it doesn't work, I will try again with tweaks and adjustments but train more and push harder.

You can't give up if you don't make it right away. If you give up on yourself and don't believe in what you can achieve, how can you expect anyone else to believe in you? I know it's gruesomely hard sometimes, but the payoff is so worth it.

When you don't have to worry about money anymore (or at least worry less), it becomes more important to know what makes you happy. It's kind of like being a kid when you didn't have to worry about bills or practical issues—you just play!

What do you want to play and do? What makes you smile? Is it painting? Is it scaling mountains? Is it travelling the world and hearing other people's stories? Is it spending time with loved ones? Is it giving back to others?

Maybe someone told you when you were younger that being happy isn't a job, and you can't do that. Perhaps they said that you'll never make money doing that or that no one wants to marry a woman that is this or that. I've heard the cruelest of things to the most simple of things, but so many are not encouraging.

Screw those haters, and put your mind on your game. Success comes with its own rewards. When you don't have to worry about money, you can do what's in your heart and soul. You don't have to worry about doing what pays the bills. You can do what pays and feeds your soul, mind, and spirit instead.

My personal goals now that I've reached this level in my life and career is to be the best version of myself. I want to explore, enjoy life, and make magic. I want to be filled with ideas and give ideas to those around me that propel them toward their dreams. I want everyone to strive toward the best version of themselves that they can be. I believe we owe ourselves and each other those blessings.

I also want to be an example for women. I don't know the exact statistics on advertising, but let's say we are bombarded with two million messages or images per day. If some of these images are not serving or helpful to the superhero women they want to be, then their dreams can quickly be extinguished. So many women and young people have so much good in them, and we're here to do so much more than we do. So why suffocate that and not let it flourish?

I want to be a part of helping women to shine and know that they can do more. I don't want them to shy away from it just because it's not the norm. I feel we should take charge and surge forward to whatever belief(s) rock our souls. I love those signs or T-shirts that say something along the lines of "She

Shepreneur

needed a hero so she became one" or "I am a woman, what's your superpower?"

When I was young, I had a T-shirt that read, "I want to be just like Barbie—that bitch has everything." I didn't take it as, "Screw you, spoiled Barbie!" To me, it meant that she had everything, and good for her because I wanted to do the same.

Only I wouldn't need a Ken because I knew I could conquer the world on my own. Perhaps I'd have a sidekick, but my success would not be given to me by the sidekick.

Chapter 4

Realism

If the Shoe Fits, Do Up the Laces

Don't run and hide from who you are.

So now you know that I worked hard, saved some money, invested in my first house, and then a spa, sold the house, closed the spa and sold off its remnants, lost a lot of money, made a lot of mistakes, tried to figure out what the hell I wanted to do with my life, settled in real estate, and continued working three jobs while I upped my real estate game.

In other words, I didn't walk straight into my current position or bank account. I failed more than a few times along the way.

My dad was always trying to teach me lessons through examples and would also give me books he had written to me in journals of lessons on life. When I was eleven years old, I was in Sanibel Island, Florida, on a trip with my family on spring break. A man came up to me and said, "Your dad wants to see you at the spa." The spa was located over a multitude of bridges far off in this jungle area that I had been to before. I shrugged and agreed, not questioning anything.

I went by myself, past the hanging trees filled with spiders and flowing water lurking with who knows what, maybe crocodiles or alligators. I carelessly strolled along for about ten minutes into the depths of the mini jungle toward the spa.

When I got there, I saw my six-foot-two slender father standing there (who was probably 150 pounds soaking wet), who said, "You failed."

"Failed what?" Then I quickly realized what my father had done and why I had failed. I was a straight-A student and go-getter who never liked to do anything wrong or be tricked, so my heart instantly sank.

My dad said, "You let some random stranger tell you that your dad wanted to see you. You have no idea who you could have been meeting out here or if they even knew your dad. You could have been kidnapped—or worse."

(Lesson learned, Dad.)

Realism means figuring out what's real, particularly with yourself. In the example above, I learned that I am a trusting person. I eventually learned that if I wanted to get somewhere in life, I should pay more attention to reality and the full picture, or the fine print.

Even today, I can be too trusting. I always choose to see the good in people, and I want them to be the best version of themselves. If they're not living their best lives, then I've been known to take them under my wing and dig deep into their mind and soul and push them to explore and find their greatness. I want to see them rid themselves of old habits that aren't serving them anymore.

The problem with this is that I have dated them, and they fall in love with me when they believe that no one has ever cared about them in this way. However, in most cases (okay, who am I kidding—in *all* of these cases), they're not at a level that propels me, and eventually, they bring me down. My body will start rejecting the relationship since it knows I'm not true to myself, and we inevitably break up.

I never think people have ulterior motives. I assume they're as good as their word, and sometimes they're not. I don't have a set way of helping people, but I like to spoil the people I date. I've bought a car for a staff member and paid them way over above the standard rate. I've treated people to excessive trips, let others live in my rentals for free, furnished people's homes at my cost, given them jobs and money—and more. Whether I've dated them or hired them, I've been screwed over many times by my generosity.

Like you, I am a work in progress. But at least I'm now aware of who I am and what my challenges are.

Face your fears.

When you face yourself, naturally, you will be confronted by your fears too. Keep in mind that they're only your fears because you've decided it is so. If you choose to make them your bitch or propelling driving force, then that's what they are, and you can conquer them.

If the idea of making these changes causes you to think and squirm, then you're getting at something good that most likely needs to be explored. Living in the "norm" doesn't scare most people; that's why it's normal. Stepping outside of fear and going for the great might scare you, but I guarantee it's worth it!

Even before I had a realtor, I would make lists of homes and drive by them all and look from the front before contacting a realtor. I would imagine what I would do to the property, such as what I would knock out or add. I would survey the rents in that area to see what the norm was and what I could expect. I guess you could say I was envisioning.

Finally, I stopped listening to the horror stories and decided to become a landlord after two things happened.

First, I had conditionally purchased a semidetached home with two units. My stepmom and her realtor friend accompanied me to the home inspection, and her friend said she wouldn't touch the property with a hundred-foot pole and suggested I back out of the deal. Being younger and feeling the need to respect and listen to my elders, I did back out.

This woman was in real estate, so she did know more than others in my circle, but I later found out that she owned a brokerage with twelve agents, and together, they sold only ten houses a year. She was by no means an expert, and there were days in my career where I sold that many homes myself in a single week.

The house she advised me to pass on sold to someone else who sold it seven years later for $291,000 more than I had offered, and it looked to be identical and not updated.

(Insert crying face.)

Then there was another two-kitchen home, which was not in the best location. I backed out during the home inspection, and again, the house went up tremendously in value, and I didn't make that little bit of money from it each month or the big payout in the end when it resold.

In the meantime, I bought that brand-new Nissan 350Z convertible I told you about and then traded it in for a Cadillac Escalade, both of which costing me tens of thousands in depreciation.

I thought, "Boy, this is dumb. I'm losing money instead of making it. I could have made money by buying those two homes, and instead, I lost money on cars. The next time, I am going to go for it. If I lose money, then I won't be in any worse of a situation than I already am."

When I decided to buy my second rental property, it was a very transactional process for me. When you decide to buy a rental property, you don't look at it like a home you would choose for yourself or your family. Instead, you make sure it has what you need as an investor.

For example, I considered how many bedrooms were in each unit and what that would bring in for rent. My criteria are different now, but initially, I shot for a 10 percent or higher return on my money. Sometimes I got 28 percent, but if I made 10 percent or more, I was happy. If it were less, I wouldn't buy the property. I also checked if it had enough parking spots and the right space for shared coin laundry.

Shepreneur

When I was first getting started in the rental properties game, I had some cash-flow problems. In Canada, you can't refinance a property during the first year, so although I bought the house for $50,000 less than its value at the time, I couldn't get to that money. That happened to be the place where the basement apartment flooded, which meant I had to shell out a lot of money to repair that expensive and unexpected problem.

I had the outside of the house dug up and added a weeping system, a sump pump, a parging coat, and a waterproofing membrane. All the flooring had to be replaced, as well as the baseboards. Then I dealt with some grading issues to keep the water away from the house, and I had to replace the furnace and roof. This experience was enough to scare away most newbie investors.

My budget did not include a surplus to handle that massive blow as I only had the deposit saved and a teeny bit extra, but not too much. I had friends who advised me to dump the property, telling me that I was in way over my head. But I hung in there and eventually made a healthy profit—$285,000 in six years of extra cash isn't too shabby, especially when I had multiples on the go.

At this point, I had dozens of rentals. I bought one during the first year, two in the second year, two again the third, then three in the fourth, slowly buying more and more and eventually getting higher valued homes that I could rent out for more money. I had learned to listen to myself, so I didn't sell them this time and finally became the landlord I knew I could be.

Kristin Cripps

I was still bartending, which was supposed to be my college job, but after a decade out of school, I was so used to the money that I didn't want to give it up. Some of my tenants would not pay their rent, but they'd come into the bar and order rounds of shots and drinks from me, which annoyingly happened about three nights a week.

I never confronted them, as in, "Bitch, no drinks for you." They'd invariably say, "Oh, we get paid tomorrow, and we'll give you the rent we owe," or some excuse that their friend gave them fifty bucks to spend at the club because it was their birthday. I would just water down their drinks and overcharge them. Two can play at that game.

I've always been a pretty open person, and when I heard about a tea leaf reader in town, I decided to go to her. She told me if there were one hundred people in a room, I would always go to the one bad person in the bunch and try to fix them.

I said, "That's not true."

She looked at me and asked, "Really?"

(Damn it, it was true.)

My friends have called me #slumlord in the past, but I disagree with that nickname. One place we frequently went camping, we had to pay a dollar for every three minutes of lukewarm water. So it makes sense to pay for laundry in my mind; I tell my friends I'd be a true slumlord if I charged people to use their showers.

Shepreneur

There are so many undeniable pros to homeownership, and I can't imagine not being in the real estate game. Years back, a friend tried to set me up with a guy in his mid-thirties when I was around the age of twenty-four. He told me then that he would never buy a house because he thought it was the most significant waste of time and money ever. I knew immediately that the relationship was never going to work, let alone even begin.

My friend insisted that he was a great guy and started to name all his good qualities. I didn't care about any of those positives if he didn't believe in homeownership. Who the heck doesn't believe in buying property besides people who can't afford it? She thought I was silly to blow him off because of his real estate views.

I didn't agree. I have dated many people who didn't own, but at least they were open to owning at some point. I could never be in a relationship with anyone against homeownership, a definite relationship no-go for me.

Not that buying and selling real estate has all been easy. I've had plenty of challenges with buying, selling, and certainly when dealing with tenants.

My first tenants paid $2,300 all-inclusive per month and supplemented that rent by having roommates. Then they said they didn't want roommates and asked me if I had anything less expensive. I moved them to my other rental, where they continued to pay for a while then eventually fell behind.

They moved out because they couldn't afford even the cheaper place, and both returned to live in their parents' homes. He called me and swore up and down he would repay me every cent he owed. I said it was nice he was going to pay me back and that I appreciated it because, in reality, he could not pay me back, and I wouldn't know where he had gone.

He said, "Pardon?" and I naively repeated myself. I never heard from him again, and he never repaid me. I screwed myself there and gave him an out he hadn't even considered.

However, this didn't turn me off renters. I was still making money at the place where they used to live. There was an upper and lower unit, so although they had fallen behind, I still had the other renters helping to pay the principal down while the house went up in value. I re-rented their unit and kept the home for six or seven years after I was stiffed.

When I first started renting to people, I chatted with them in a friendly way, never letting on that I owned the property. I found it beneficial for them to think I was acting as the landlord or property manager rather than an owner. Then I could blame things on the owner, such as when I served the renters notice for late rent, not agreeing to their request to paint the walls a particular colour, having an above-ground pool that would kill the grass, or allowing their boyfriend or girlfriend and three kids to move in.

When tenants knew I owned the property, they'd think I was easygoing, wouldn't give them a hard time, or that if I liked them, I would let them be late with their rent. But when I was just following the owner's requests, they understood and didn't take it out on me.

I don't have any regrets about being a landlord, aside from not getting into it sooner. I have never been an aggressive investor, so I could have bought more and been actively searching for other homes to buy, but because I was so busy in my daily job and life, acquiring new properties was a very backburner thing.

I earn income from selling real estate and from my real estate investments. Plus, now I am a paid speaker. However, I don't see a time when I won't be involved in real estate, whether that's buying, renovating, flipping, converting properties, or changing uses. I have said many times that I eat, sleep, and breathe real estate, and it's true.

When you commit to something, realize you are above nothing.

Did I want to deal with lower-class renters on a high volume my whole life? Nope, big negative there; however, I knew the lower-priced properties were stepping-stones to higher-priced properties.

You can't say that you want to look like a person with crazy abs and hardly any body fat and just snap your fingers, and it happens. It took years for your body to get the way it is, and it takes a lot of determination, hard work, and sacrifice to make those improvements to get to another shape and appearance. Real estate is no different.

For example, I bought a disgusting thirteen-bedroom rooming house, which I should have bulldozed, but I didn't, and it cost me more in the long run than if I had just torn it down. There was a toothless tenant who looked to be in his midseventies but was probably in his late thirties and had just lived a rough life. He said to me, "If I knew a pretty lady was coming over, I would have cleaned up a bit."

There was no cleaning the house, though, unless someone had a shovel and gas mask. These men were going number 2 in the sump pump, which (if you are not familiar with a sump pump) is not a toilet, so the smell was horrific. But I enjoy buying ugly things and making them pretty, so I took on the job. I made it into three apartments and made a "cash cow" out of it, as the saying goes.

I never liked buying pretty properties nor ever purchased them unless it was the odd time for me to live in the home, but that happens rarely.

I acquired my favorite of all my properties thus far in my early thirties. My client sent me a listing, and I thought, "Ew, why are we going to look at this one?" Nevertheless, I drove the half hour up the highway to show her this waterfront property. She was considering buying it with her friend as they were similar ages with adult-aged children who no longer lived at home. Since it had two kitchens, it would save them on their mortgage to split the house.

The property was massive, with five acres on the water and overgrown like nobody's business. It probably hadn't been updated since 1975. I'm pretty sure you flushed four or five bucks down the drain every time you flushed the toilet as the tanks were so big. The bathroom had a chocolate brown bathtub, sink, and toilet.

Eleven days before closing, she called me and asked, "What if we can't get financing?"

I said, "Well, they're going to sue you, me, and the brokerage, why?"

She explained that the gentleman she was going to share accommodations with had declared bankruptcy before and not told her, and she couldn't get the whole mortgage on her own.

Then I learned that there were more issues and that the property was difficult to finance, but I told my clients I would take over her agreement so she wouldn't end up in a lawsuit. I had around twenty-two properties at that time and had no idea if I could even get a mortgage. I was determined to figure it out, but it turned out I couldn't figure it out. I hadn't done my taxes in a couple of years, and I owed some money on my visa card. Plus, the lender didn't like the property because it had a septic system, was zoned recreational, and there were five lots in total.

The lender said they would mortgage the one lot with the house, but I needed to buy the other four lots outright. So I rented out the house where I had lived with a saltwater pool and no neighbours behind and moved into the house with the brown toilet. It was the worst out of all my homes, both current and past. I thought I would renovate it and live on the water, buy a stand-up paddleboard and not work as much, but I soon realized that it was a pain living out of town, and I moved back as quickly as I could.

Later, I took out a regular mortgage after needing a private at 10 percent interest for one year. Then I was able to start developing on the lots and eventually tore down the house I had been living in. I will be short term renting all seventeen units that are being built. Two are completed so far, and I am making lots of Instagram spots for people to post so other people want to come there and pose as opposed to renting at the neighbouring short-term competition properties.

Whenever something happens, there's always a lesson, a story, or someone you are supposed to meet.

Thinking positively and striving pay tenfold, not only in situations, but also in life. But job-wise, you never know who you're going to run across. But if they see you slacking and hating life and your job, do you think they're going to offer you a role in their better establishment? I think not. I love the stories of life and am always open to whatever the day or journey brings me. Perhaps that's why I love to travel so much: there are so many lessons, adventures, and stories to be had.

I had some tenants renting other rooms out to people to help pay their rent, which was smart, but some of those rooms were not bedrooms as they did not have windows.

A friend asked, "What if they die in a fire?"

I called my insurance company and asked the question, and they said, "We would rebuild the house. However, if their family members or their insurance sued you for a million or three million, that would not be covered because those aren't real bedrooms."

Stupidly, instead of adding windows, which I've done many times since then, I sold the bungalow. I worried that I was going to get sued, so I sold it. But I should have just added the windows, kept that house, and I would have had an extra $400,000 in equity.

But I was in my listening-to-too-many-other-people phase and not to the people that have experience in real estate. I wasn't listening to the right people. I was still buying and selling at that point and keeping an arrangement of everything. But I was not yet in the let's-just-add-windows phase, so I stupidly also sold that bungalow.

Do things for the little pain and significant gain.

I never rented rooms out in my own home; I always put in second units. I grew up as an only child, and although I have stepbrothers and stepsisters, they never lived in the same house as me. My parents were gone thirteen or fourteen hours a day, so I was accustomed to being by myself.

Living in a house with four or five other people and sharing the same kitchen is not my idea of a good time. Shoot me now. I'm not used to that noise. I'm not saying that's not an excellent way to make money because I have lots of friends that rent out parts of their home. But my approach was always to put another apartment in so they have their separate kitchen, bathroom, entrance, and laundry.

That was always the first thing I did. If it didn't have an apartment, I would add one. Whether I had to add a separate entrance, or it was a raised bungalow, and I had to block off some walls and add a door, I did so. Raised bungalows or a walkout basement are good, so it's brighter downstairs. The house I live in right now is divided in half. Neither of us is in the basement, though, because it's an old basement and not habitable, or I'd put a third unit downstairs.

I divided the house in half, and even though I could have retired years ago, I don't need to have somebody else paying rent—but why not have somebody else pay $18,000 rent per year? My mortgage is low, about $670 a month. Why not have that?

People say, "But I don't want to rent out parts of my home."

I ask, "Why not? Why do you not want to live for free?"

People also say, "You're so lucky, you go on vacation so much. You're seeing all these new places and having so much fun." But then they don't want to make sacrifices I do to have those things.

A close friend of mine took time off this past summer. She applied for a job where she worked and didn't get it, so she was upset and decided to take nine weeks off.

She hadn't had a summer off since she was a young teenager. She took time off, and I asked, "Instead of going back full time, why don't you rent out part of your house?"

Their house has a side door. There's a door completely blocking off her kitchen on the main floor, and right at the bottom of the stairs is a laundry room. I said, "You don't have to change plumbing or anything. All you have to do is add a little wet bar area kitchen for renters. You could rent that for $1,900 to $2,000 a month, inclusive. That helps supplement your income if you want to take every single Friday off plus take a trip here and there."

She said, "No, we don't want anybody in our space."

I don't need anybody next door to me either, but why not? I don't care. I've never had them specifically in my space because that doesn't work with me. But I don't think that's not an option. It just depends on your personality. I don't like it for my character as I enjoy my own space, which is why I have always had multiunit households to pay my mortgage.

That's why I save that money, so I live for free, plus the house goes up in value. Then I can refinance and keep going house after house after house.

There are many ways to save money to buy a house. You could rent a room. Some people will say they don't want to share a bathroom or a kitchen, but it's not forever. If you ever want to get ahead in life, you might have to make some small sacrifices in the interim for long-term gain.

Rent out a room. If you bring in $550, then that's an instant $9,000 a year you'll save compared to the person renting the full one bedroom basement apartment that doesn't have the option to rent out any part of their rental. Plus, your bedroom could be up on the second floor instead of the dungeon.

Or you could rent a four-bedroom house for $1,700 a month, and if you approximate $300 a month for utilities and split it with your friends, each person will pay $500. Do that with a bunch of couples or somewhere where utilities are included, or rent is a bit cheaper because the upgrades are nonexistent, or the area is not the greatest and save even more.

Or you could take on a part-time second job, or hell, have two or three jobs as I did. It's not a forever thing people: suck it up.

The question to ask yourself is, "How bad do I want it?"

Chapter 5

Accountability

Put Some Lipstick On, or Take a Shit

This quote is courtesy of the mother of one of my childhood friends. She said, "Honey, if life isn't going your way, there are only and always two ways to solve it. Put some lipstick on, or take a shit."

Learning about accountability—taking a shit.

In the spring of 2018, I attended a real estate conference in California. I'd heard the realtor speaking on stage before, but he seemed completely different this time. Afterward, I asked him what he'd changed and why he came across so differently. He told me that he'd done Landmark, NLP, and had attended some Tony Robbins courses.

My personality is such that I looked them up that day to book them all. Well, the NLP didn't work with my schedule. I had watched Tony Robbins a million times on YouTube and seen him live twice, but there was a Landmark course with an opening the following weekend, so Landmark it was.

Since the speaker is a bigwig realtor in San Diego, I assumed it was a real estate seminar, so I signed up, booked my short-term rental, and never Googled the course to see what it was about. Well, (gulp) the course was not about real estate at all, but a

Shepreneur

deep dive into your subconscious patterns, life, childhood, old thoughts, and stories to free you to live your best life today.

I was bawling on the first and second day of the event, thinking that this wasn't at all about fucking real estate—sob, sob, snot, snot—but figured it had aligned with me so I must have been meant to be there. The course lasted for an intense three twelve to fourteen-hour days with homework every night and on each break.

I, however, was not doing the homework and instead chose to catch up on my phone and emails on breaks while trying not to be a basket case in the little bit of evening that remained after the emotional roller-coaster days.

I was sitting in a stairwell on the second day on my phone doing real estate things (and not my homework) when a lady who worked/volunteered there approached me and said, "I can't help but notice that you're not doing your assignment." I smiled politely and returned my eyes to my screen and thought, *Fuck off, lady. You're cutting into my lunch break, and you have no idea how much work I have to do.*

When she walked away, I put down my phone and leaned my head against the cold concrete wall, realizing I would always be behind on my phone, and maybe I should try out this whole homework assignment stuff they were requesting. I pulled out the paper I had folded into six squares and started to do the assignment.

First, I called a realtor who'd been a family friend. He'd been around our house from the time I was aged ten to sixteen, and I used to babysit his kids. I'd seen him multiple times a week for years in my home and at various family functions. When I was sixteen years old, he did something inappropriate to me, and I'd carried tremendous hate for him for decades. I hadn't seen him since the incident and didn't want to. (I think I would have Lorena Bobbitt'd him if I'd had the chance.)

When I was working as a massage therapist, I'd massaged his wife, not knowing who she was as it had been so long since I'd seen them. During her massage, she mentioned that he was in the reception area, waiting for his massage. My blood started to boil, and I did not want to see him.

I went to the back instead of the front, to avoid seeing him in the waiting room. I called the receptionist from the back phone and asked who my next client was. She told me his name, and I said, "That massage is *not* fucking happening." I told her that I would explain if she wanted to know, but I was not massaging him—not today, not tomorrow, and not ever.

So during the course, I had to call him. My heart was racing as I dialed his number, but his wife answered the phone and said he was out walking their dog. Since I was a realtor by then, I felt comfortable leaving a message that it was Kristin from X Realty. We played telephone tag but eventually spoke.

On the phone, I told him that I was taking a course and that I had hated him for a long time. I said that I never wanted to be a realtor because I associated all realtors with scumbags. I said I'd released those feelings and that I wasn't mad anymore, and I hoped that he, the boys, and his wife were well.

Shepreneur

"I'm not sure if your stepdad told you, but I had a car accident," he said. I didn't know if he was telling me this to elicit sympathy or if he was telling me this to say he had a brain injury and didn't know who I was. So I asked why he was telling me.

He said he knew who I was but had no idea why I'd hated him for so long and why I had avoided Christmas and Thanksgiving events he attended. I wasn't going to let him off the hook so quickly in my eyes, so I told him what had happened between us. He said he felt sick to his stomach and wanted to vomit.

It rang a bell, he said, but he thought I was older. But that wasn't true. He knew my exact age because right before the incident, he'd asked me what was new, and I'd told him that it would be my birthday that Saturday. He'd asked me how old I was turning, and I told him, so his copout didn't fly.

Anyway, I told him I was no longer angry and invited him to the graduation night of the course to make amends, but he said they were going to be at their cottage. He thanked me for calling and wished me well.

Learning about accountability—putting on lipstick.

Part of my coursework involved calling my mom to tell her that I knew she had a baby she'd given up for adoption and that I wanted to meet my sister. Whew! That was a big one.

Since I was ten, I'd known that I had a half sister. I was watching a talk show, Sally Jessy Raphael, or Montel Williams, and they were reuniting people that had been given up for adoption and hence never met. They'd be reunited and run across the stage, bawling their eyes out (I'm sure you know the drill). I was sitting on the floor, and my dad was sitting on one chair, and my stepmother was on another. I looked back at my dad and asked, "Are we missing anyone?"

He paused and said, "Well," and then my stepmother interrupted and said, "John, it's not your place to tell." I started crying because I didn't know what was going on. I knew I wasn't adopted because I look too much like my parents, but I was still confused and upset. He then told me that before he met my mom in university, she had had a daughter and given her up for adoption. I never told my mom that I knew, and that is how I left it for twenty-six years—a secret I knew.

My parents were very conservative, and they never talked about sex. After I left home, I lived with a boyfriend here and there, and when we visited my mom for Christmas or Thanksgiving, she would make my boyfriend sleep in the basement, and I'd sleep on the second floor. I'd say, "But we live together and sleep in the same bed at home," but they'd say, "Well, not here you don't." This was not a topic that was up for discussion.

I took my mom to Paris, not too long before she went through radiation treatment for breast cancer. (Both my mom and stepmom had cancer, one breast, one lymphoma.) It was a lovely trip where we visited four countries. It was so beautiful to be walking along the river and see her get teary. I've only seen her tear up one other time in my life, and it hadn't yet happened, so that was the first time.

My mom said that she was so happy because she never thought she'd make it to Paris. Of course, it's wonderful that she's healthy now and can explore parts of the world she has never visited. But at the time, it was a bonding thing for me to feel and experience with her.

As a child, you don't realize how much your parents give up to take care of you, so to give her some joy back was a great feeling—love you, Mom!

I tried to coerce her in various ways to confess I had a sister, which didn't work. I also tried one other time previously when I took her to Vegas for Mother's Day and tried to get her drunk, but that didn't work either. On both occasions, I was too chicken to blurt it out.

During the trip to Paris, I kept slyly working on her about my sister. I started by saying, "It's a girls' trip, so you have to tell me something I don't already know about you."

But Mom didn't give up the goods.

Next, I suggested that we play truth or dare.

But nope, silence.

I told her how my friend and her mom had gone to a Cher concert, and my friend told her mom that she'd had an abortion, and her mom shared that she'd given a child up for adoption. They bonded and ended up meeting the brother and how wonderful it was. I hoped that sharing their story would push my mom to tell me.

No luck there either.

Then I tried alcohol, and when Mom said, "Oh my, this drink is strong, and it's making me tipsy." I waved the waiter over and asked for another one, but still no luck. I was too nervous to ask her directly about my sister then, and perhaps it wasn't the right time.

According to my dad, my mom had said she'd tell me about my sister when I was twelve years old and old enough to understand. Then she moved the date to when I was thirteen, later fourteen, and finally sixteen. But then I moved out, and our relationship became rocky, so she never talked to me about my sister.

It had never before been the right time to press my mom about my sister. Because we'd had a strained relationship for quite some time, I was afraid it would go back to that if I confronted her about giving up a baby for adoption. I was on tippy-toes because it took some time to get back to our current healthy mother-daughter relationship, and I wanted to maintain a good relationship with her.

Being an only child, I was so interested in this girl/woman out there in the world. I wondered if we had any similarities. Could we have unknowingly crossed paths already?

I didn't know much about her. I thought she was born when my mom was fourteen or fifteen, but my mom had been sixteen years old. I thought she was adopted in Oakville, but she was born in Toronto and adopted in Hamilton. I have a different last name from my mom, and with so many missing pieces to the puzzle, our meeting just wasn't lining up.

Shepreneur

I had once asked my late grandma's best friend, as I learned from my dad that she had followed my sister's life a bit and knew where she lived and went to school. However, she said, "Angela [my mother] is the only piece left of Renate [my late grandmother] that I have, and I can't jeopardize our relationship by telling you."

I was determined to see if my sister looked like me as she is the only person who shares a parent with me. To give you an idea of how determined I was, I used to interrogate people discreetly at the resort where I massaged. I wanted to see if they came from the area where I believed that my sister was adopted if they looked to be in a similar age range. I wanted to know if I could get out of them that they were adopted, then I'd look at their features and see if I thought it could be a possibility.

I'm a creeper, I know.

Even though I was afraid to confront my mom, when I saw so many people in that course who had held onto things for decades longer than I had, I thought, "Fuck this. I'm not holding onto this shit forever. I don't want to be crying up there when I'm eighty-two or eighty-eight years old about what I wished I would have done."

Some family members of the attendees had passed away. The people onstage were writing letters or pretending they were having a conversation with the person who had passed. I didn't want to do that; I wanted to have the conversation while it was possible.

Experiencing all the sharing by people in the course made me realize I didn't want to hold onto things and let them take over my life as it had with them. So I picked up the phone to call my mother, as we were told not to text, WhatsApp, or email—we had to speak on the phone.

I was happy when I reached my mom's voicemail; though even that was breaking the rules, it was a massive step forward for me. Unfortunately—or maybe fortunately—my mom's voicemail only allows callers to talk for one minute and then disconnects.

I had to keep calling back because I couldn't cram everything I wanted to say into sixty seconds. On my third call, my mom picked up. Because I'd called three times, my stepdad thought it must have been an emergency and told her I kept calling while she'd been in the garden.

I said that everything was fine, but I was at a course in Toronto where we were learning not to keep secrets. I said that I knew I had a sister as she'd given up a child for adoption and that I wanted to meet her. At first, my mom was mad that my dad had told me. I said it doesn't matter that he told me; I want to find her. After a few short comments, I said I had to run back into class.

I became swamped with work in the following weeks. My mom and I hadn't talked about my sister since my call from Landmark. Then my mom called a few weeks later to say that she'd applied through some program and had learned her daughter's name.

Shepreneur

It was a Sunday evening, and I was at home, and I instantly started to cry. Mom said, "I knew you'd cry," and when I asked if she did, she said that she hadn't. I think growing up in a strict German household taught her not to show emotion or feelings.

I didn't know what to expect with my sister, because I didn't know what her dad looked like. I have crept things, as my mom had yearbooks, so I used to creep the yearbooks and look at what people would write to see if I could figure out who the guy was. My dad didn't know the guy's name and told me that my mom went on one date with the guy when she was in grade nine.

He was in grade thirteen and a captain of the football team. They had sex one time, and it was her first time. She got pregnant, and he pretended he didn't know her. That wasn't the story, but that's what I had thought it was.

As this was the story that I knew, it helped me when I was younger because I was standoffish with guys. I thought they just wanted to get in my pants, so I kept guys away. I was the last of all my friends, by far, to lose my virginity because I was afraid of what happened to my mom, to be left and pretended that the date never happened. I think my mom didn't tell me about her past because she thought I'd say, "You did it too. You can't stop me from having a kid as a teenager."

During my earlier creeping stage, one of the signatures in my mother's yearbook read, "Firetrucks are red, cop cars are blue, come over tonight, and boy, will I fuck you."

I showed her and asked, "Mom, who is this?"

She said, "I don't know who that is. I have never seen him in my life. Who wrote that in there?" She was very defensive.

Being in real estate, I can look up anyone, and if they own a home, I can find their address. When we learned my sister's name, I went straight to my computer. Luckily for us, she had not changed her name to her married name as that is quite a common name, but she was the only one in all of Ontario!

I also typed in her name on Facebook, and only one came up. I did the same thing on Instagram and Google, and my mom and I continued creeping her while we were on the phone together. Now that we had her name, we were able to learn a lot about her online.

We learned that she was married to a man but had no kids. They seemed to travel a lot and had two dogs, a niece, and a nephew. Also, from Google, I could see where she worked and where she had attended university.

I have super dark hair, and I saw that Lynda has blonde hair, as does our mom. In my head, I thought she would look more like me than she does, but I was still happy to see all the stuff about her online and that she was smiling in so many pictures, and that she was a traveler. Then I was shocked that she didn't have kids.

I thought for sure she'd have children, being eleven years older than me, but she didn't. Lynda had dogs, which I liked because I would pick dogs over cats any day. Even though I love all animals, I'm a dog person. I learned that she grew up as an only child when I read her mother's obituary, which said that she was a mother to Lynda, not a mother to Lynda, Josh, and Sam, etc.

My mom reached out to her on Facebook but didn't receive an answer, so she said, "I don't think she wants us in her life." I explained that there was a special place where messages go when people aren't friends with the sender. I never look in mine and didn't even know it existed until recently. We figured she might not have yet seen our mother's message.

My mom said, "Maybe she's busy with her own life and wonders where I've been all her life and hates me." I said that could be the case; however, it also could be that she just didn't see the message, so we shouldn't make such drastic assumptions.

We learned that Lynda lived about an hour and a half from us, which put her smack dab in the middle of my mom and me. I suggested that my mom write her a letter, and if she didn't respond, then I would knock on her door.

My mom felt I shouldn't go to her door, and that if she didn't respond, then we should assume she doesn't want to talk to us. I said that the letter could get lost in the mail, and if she didn't want to meet us, then she could tell me to my face, and I would leave her alone.

Yes, I am persistent.

So my mom sent my sister a letter with her phone number, and my sister called her. My mom was ecstatic.

We learned that Lynda had also grown up in a German family, like our mom, and lived right near me in Hamilton. She'd worked at a Dairy Queen across the street from my school, which I had stopped at every single school day. I had big ears, but my mom wanted me to wear my hair up so I wouldn't get lice at school. Because I hated my ears, I'd stop every day at that Dairy Queen and take my hair down, using their restroom mirror.

Lynda also worked at Northern Reflections, which was the only store I knew of that carried double zero pants that fit me. When I was a kid and still living at home, we were frequenting her two jobs on regular occasions without even knowing who she was. Her mother had passed ten years before we found her, and her adopted dad is still alive today. I've met him, but since he has dementia, he doesn't grasp the whole concept.

When my mom told Lynda who her biological father was, we discovered that he'd worked for thirty years at the university Lynda attended. Once Lynda and her father were connected, he asked my sister if she'd gone to her graduation and did the typical walk across the stage, handshake, pose for pictures, and walk offstage. She had, so that meant that every year he'd been there (which overlapped her time), he'd been the person onstage shaking the graduate's hands.

My sister had shaken her father's hand and looked him in the eye and had never even known it!

It makes me feel good because this all happened because of a course I took. I go to tons of courses every year (I'm a course junkie). I love that my wanting to expand myself helped other people and my family, as opposed to being only about my well-being and business, which is the case in most of my courses. It changed our lives completely, which is something I could never have imagined.

It completely changed my mom as well.

She said, "I love you," to me in my late twenties for the first time, and I said, "Pardon me, what? Sorry, what did you say?"

My mom is ordinarily quite closed. You know how some people hug so tight and squeeze like they're huggers? Well, my mom will have a foot and a half between us and tap us over quickly on the back and be done with it. Now she seems free, like a different person, and she gives real hugs and shows her emotions.

My sister, my mom, and I went to New York for her birthday in April, and it was like she was with her two best friends. She was giddy like a kid in a candy shop; she was absolutely over the moon.

My sister and mom see each other a couple of times a week. My mom will stay at my sister's house for two to three nights, and my sister will stay over at our mom's as well. They've bonded so much, and I am truly grateful. I think they both enjoy their newfound family.

I think if my mom had told me about my sister when I was fourteen years old, and we reached out to her at that point, my sister's adoptive mother would have still been alive. My sister might have said, "Thank you, but I have my own family." I don't know why it wasn't supposed to come together before, but it didn't. I feel that it all came together in the way and at the time it was supposed to.

I felt a little bad that Lynda didn't have children since I didn't give my mom grandchildren either. But I am so happy she's in our lives, and my mom has become a different person since she has come into our lives.

Thank you, Lynda! You are our angel through and through!

It's never too late to get started.

I ran into a friend's mom recently, and she told me she planned to sell her house and rent in the future. She said not to tell her daughter, but she barely had any money, and because she's made some poor decisions, when she sells the house, she will be lucky to break even. This confession saddened me quite a bit because she's in her seventies and still working. I don't think she can afford to stop working or make enough to stay in a nursing home when that time should come.

It made me think of my grandma Omi, my favourite of all favourites. Business-wise, we were complete opposites. I wish she had not passed so early in my life for many reasons, but specifically, it would have been nice to spoil her so she would not have to work anymore. I would have also liked to have had the chance to show her how she could get ahead in life and not live paycheque to paycheque.

Omi worked as a receptionist at a doctor's office and paid a lofty rent in Oakville, a posh community about thirty minutes west of Toronto on the waterfront. She didn't have money for dentists and regular maintenance and cleanings and eventually started to lose her teeth.

Shepreneur

Due to a lack of funds—and even though she worked at a doctor's office—she would put Krazy Glue on one end of her tooth and shove it back in. It baffles me to think about it because I can't understand how she could do that. She used to pay me three dollars to dye, cut, and perm her hair, which was a score for me because that was a lot of money to me and huge savings for her—a win-win for both of us.

Both these ladies—my friend's mom and Omi—didn't have a pot to piss in between them, if you'll pardon the expression. The fact that they both had so much unused potential saddens me.

I want everyone to live their best life. Life is short, and saying it and realizing it and going after it are completely different things. I believe we are on earth more than once (but usually only remember once), so we need to make the most of it.

You shouldn't think, "It's too late for me. I'm too old now."

That's BS!

You need to give your head a shake, or it really will be too late, and you'll go down that rabbit hole of shame and guilt.

For example, at a course, I met a lady in her mid-eighties, and she had never done any schooling after she'd left high school. She shared that her mom had told her that boys didn't like smart girls—boys liked pretty girls. She had it stuck in her head that if she were too bright, men wouldn't like her. She ended up going to university at the age of eighty-six!

She'd always wanted to learn psychology and get her degree, and so that's what she did. She graduated and is conquering old beliefs left, right, and centre lately. Good for her!

I'm glad she finally decided to rewire her thought process and scrap her mother's ridiculous way of thinking and do what she wanted. Most of the time, our parents have done the best job they could do to raise us, but that doesn't mean that what worked for them—as well as their thought patterns, ideas, and ideals—will work for us.

Chapter 6

Enjoyment

Do What You Love

Don't get to the end of your life and realize you should have done it differently. Why not say, "What an incredible fucking trip! Hells to the ya. Peace out!"

Each of us is different. Your passion is not random, so I encourage you to go after the things that light *you* up. For example, I shop, and I love decorating and designing the houses I renovate. I take salsa dancing lessons and Spanish lessons. I go to the gym, do my real estate transactions, and renovate homes. I eat lots of sushi and see my friends and travel: this is what lights me up.

I enjoy spoiling my nephews and niece. For example, one time, I had my two nephews with me at a store before we headed out for three days of fun and spending money on anything and everything they wanted.

The younger nephew asked if it was okay if he bought this or that. I said, "Yes, Sam, I told you, you could get whatever you want."

He asked, "Why?"

I replied, "Why not?" His eyes lit up, and he screamed as if he had just been injected with the biggest hit of sugar.

Shepreneur

Many people say that being a grandparent is better than being a parent, and I used to wonder why. Now I know. If I were the parent, I probably wouldn't spoil my nephews and niece as I do, much less have the energy to do cool things with them so often. Since I see them occasionally, I can be the "fun aunt," and I enjoy that role.

Being an aunt is like a younger, hipper version of a grandparent—no offense, grandparents, you're still pretty rad!

I also enjoy dance, and it really lights me up. As a kid, I did jazz, tap, ballet, lyrical, musical theater, and acro. I took classes five days a week and competed during the other two days each week. Every day after school, I'd walk from school to the studio, and then my mom would pick me up after my classes.

I stopped dancing when I moved out because I couldn't afford to keep up with the lessons. I had to enter competitions in order to teach, but to do competitions, I had to take five classes a week.

Therefore, I'd have to pay to do five other classes, pay for five other costumes, and pay to enter those competitions just to make a bit of money in return. I couldn't afford the outlay plus pay my rent, so as soon as I moved out, I stopped.

I went from 92 pounds to 120 pounds in *two* months. I had such low body fat and was working out four or five hours a day until I stopped working out at all and began working a job where I stood still as a cashier. Swipe, swipe, swipe was my only exercise.

Now I've picked up dancing again. The reason why I love salsa is that you never see anybody dancing with a sour face; when dancing, people are always happy, smiling and laughing. I believe that dancing and music can take you out of any bad mood. If you put on some uplifting music and shake your booty, you'll feel better.

Travel more; work less.

Praise the Lord, hallelujah! Yes, live your life!

Don't take only a honeymoon and a retirement vacation—get out there, explore, and see what the world has to offer. This is my philosophy, and I understand it's not everyone's cup of tea, so I don't judge if it's not yours. If someone asked during a popular game with my nephews and littles in the car, "Would you rather have no legs and continue travelling the world or have legs but never be able to go on a trip again?" I'd pick no legs and travel all over. To each his own.

I have been on dozens and dozens of trips (probably sixty to eighty-five) and have no intention of stopping. I've been all over the United States, most of Canada, Iceland, Greece, Turkey, Italy, France, Spain, Ireland, Portugal, Croatia, England, El Salvador, India, Nepal, Bhutan, Indonesia, Honduras, Thailand, Egypt, Jordan, Guatemala, Brazil, Argentina, the Caribbean, the French Polynesian islands, Chili, Uruguay, Peru, the United Arab Emirates, Holland, Norway, Finland, Tuscany, Mexico, and Ecuador.

I'm sure I'm missing a dozen, but those are the ones I can recall. I'm looking forward to seeing even more places as I continue my speaking gigs and exploration across the globe.

Shepreneur

I mentioned that I buy all the pretty things for my renovations. When I make these purchases, I do so on my visa and get points. So while I go on between four to fifteen trips a year, I have not paid for a single flight since 2008.

Feel free to reread that last sentence.

I use points on my travel visa to fund my travel; that's another reason why I buy the pretty things for my renovations.

I don't have a particular philosophy on travelling; I just like exploring the world. In Canada, I tend to work most of the time. But in other countries, I get massages, shop, wander, explore, relax, eat better, and sleep better.

I take in more, and I'm more retired when I'm away, which is why I go away so often. I love to Google image the world and zoom in and look up places and randomly pick travel destinations. I don't use a travel agent. I know it's strange and not the most practical way of doing things, but I'm the type of visually oriented person who will pick destinations based on pictures rather than paragraphs or reviews.

In addition to travel, I move homes a lot as I get bored quite quickly, and I would be a severely angry camper if I could not move for the remainder of my life. I met a couple, and he told me he was ninety-two and a half. People don't say "and a half" unless they're six years old. But he was ninety-two and a half, and his wife was eighty-nine.

The couple had lived in their house for *sixty-two* years—that's insane to me, and I would never ever do that. I don't care how beautiful or perfect it is; staying in one house would be like being in an insane asylum in a padded room with a straightjacket to me.

I could not, would not, and will not do that. (Cue Dr. Seuss.)

Shit is gonna go down when you travel.

Back when digital cameras first came out, I was on a cruise ship with my two stepbrothers, their wives, my dad, and stepmom. We had travelled for three weeks in Europe, and I had a collection of photos to show of our adventures. My dad wanted to check out my new camera, and I figured it was because he was thinking of getting a digital camera for himself.

My stepmom called me about thirty minutes later to say that my dad was playing with my camera and received a message asking if he wanted to reformat the camera, and he clicked yes—deleting our entire three weeks' worth of photos.

A sidenote to that trip was that my dog, Bailey, had chewed the corner of my passport. I'd taken six trips since then and had not encountered a single issue. This time when at the airport with six family members, two of whom had the same last name as me, the authorities said I had a defaced passport and couldn't join my family.

That was on a Saturday. My family went on to Greece while I went home and surprised my friends who were watching my dogs. I applied for an emergency passport the following Monday. Well, it turns out an emergency passport means that they call the ten people instead of the two that they make you write down. They take you to a room and phone all ten friends right in front of you. They ask your people about where you were born, your eye colour and hair colour, and so forth.

The fellow hung up the phone after making all those calls and said, "Your friends don't know where you were born, do they? I think one out of ten got it right."

I explained that I moved a lot as a kid. He said, "Do you also dye your hair a lot? A lot of your friends don't even know the real colour of your hair."

Perhaps I travel too much?

Never! There is no such thing in my world.

Don't let fear dictate your life (or your travels).

When I picked El Salvador as a travel destination, everything I read advised travelers not to go, but I had a fantastic vacation. The same thing happened in Brazil. I read about what a dangerous place it was and how you should not go unless you had to. Yet again, I had another incredible vacation. Egypt was the same. Some things you just have to experience for yourself and draw your own conclusions.

I was once in NYC with a friend, and at the subway station, we saw a group of people in a circle. We walked over and saw that someone was break-dancing in the center, so we watched for a while and then went on our way. A few days later, we were on the subway again, and again, we saw a group of people, but this time, it was a much larger group. We walked over to watch again, but this time, someone was beating someone up in the middle (insert naive Canadian girls).

On that same trip, we took the subway, all dolled up, of course. A woman said to us, "I don't know where you girls think you're going, but you're going the wrong way."

We said, "No, we're going the right way. We're going to a club."

She said, "You need to get off at the next stop and go back the way you came. This is not a good area for you, and you stand out like sore thumbs." She was right; we were going the wrong way. (Thank you, lady—whoever you were—for warning us.)

On the first day of a planned tour in Egypt, they handed us Styrofoam boxes that contained two boiled eggs, fig jam, a bun, a croissant, and a banana. On that first day, I said, "Ooh la la! Fig jam! How exotic." By the twenty-first day, however, I was like, "Ugh, someone shoot me—not the same breakfast again?!"

It was like being in a scene from *Groundhog Day*.

In Egypt, they have the Tourist and Antiquity police walking around with machine guns to keep tourists safe. I had nightmares the first three days of the month I was there, as I had never seen a machine gun before. It must have scared me since it kept creeping into my nighttime thoughts.

During that trip, I'd pocketed a butter knife from a restaurant (bad, I know, but I'm sure karma comes back around to bite me at my Airbnbs). I'd bought some Nutella and peanut butter, so I needed the knife to spread them on my croissant or bun since the plastic one they had supplied sucked.

Shepreneur

When I went to the Egyptian airport to depart, a security official said, "Ma'am, you have a knife in your bag."

Forgetting about the butter knife I'd taken, I said, "No, I don't."

"Yes, you do!" he insisted.

I was picturing a machete or something, so I kept denying I had a knife. More and more security personnel were gathering around me, and they were all chattering, "She has a knife! She has a knife!"

If I'd been in Canada or the States, I would have thought it was some hidden prank show, but in Egypt, I was concerned. I thought that perhaps I hadn't watched my bag closely enough, and someone had slipped a machete inside.

Fuck, this isn't good.

When they finally removed the butter knife from my bag, I was instantly relieved, as I forgot I had it. But security didn't appear to be as happy as I felt and continued to look at me like the danger they thought I was. I showed them the Nutella and peanut butter and tried to explain the knife was for spreading those products. Once the concern was resolved at the airport, I did not go to Egyptian jail and was allowed to return to Canada.

Whew.

Be flexible.

I almost wiped out my friend and me in Bermuda. (I am returning there this summer for her wedding, so look out, motorists!) I was driving the scooter on the other side of the road, and I didn't like leaning into corners. It was probably about four days into our vacation, and I was getting more used to speed. We were going around a corner, not leaning in when our speed took us across the other lane of traffic, up a curb, and we wobbled all over the place.

My friend put her foot down for balance, which ripped her sandal off, but we survived. I'm not sure how we didn't tip over or crash, to be honest. On the other side of the half wall where we had stopped was a drop-off to a market below, which is where we would have landed.

She instantly started videoing and said, "You saved me! You saved me! We almost died on this corner, but this girl saved me." (I was thinking more like I almost killed us). She said, "I'll buy you a drink tonight for saving my life." My heart was beating a million beats a minute.

During a trip to India, our train was about eight hours late. Darkness fell, and we'd been advised to avoid being out once the sun had set. There was supposed to be a person who would pick us up, and we were supposed to know him by the sign he held with our names. We had a creepy fellow on the train harassing us, so my friend started crying and said she wanted to contact the embassy.

When the guy who picked us up didn't have an ID, we wondered if he'd just taken the sign from the real driver and was going to murder us or take us to some brothel. When you're in a flight-or-fight response for so long, sometimes your nerves get the best of you.

Take opportunities where you find them.

In Turkey, I found a white knock-off Prada purse that I really wanted, as I used to like bags back then. Being a barterer through and through, and since that was the first store I went in, I thought thousands of other shops would have an identical purse. Unfortunately, the store owner was right, and no one else had that exact bag.

Damnit!

I sent my stepmom back in, as I didn't want him having the joy that he was right, but he said, "You Texas mom! You Texas mom! See, she no find!" (I was wearing a long skirt and a cowboy buckle belt and white tank top and cowboy hat, hence the "you Texas mom" comment.)

I got the purse but didn't get it for the deal I wanted: bartering fail.

(Oh, and please don't judge my outfit. I worked at a country bar at that time, so the whole ambiance had rubbed off on me a bit.)

When I was in Croatia, I got a free photoshoot (insert pat on the back). There were professional photographers at the seminar I was attending, but they charged 450 USD per half hour. Um yeah, hells to the no! Are you on drugs? They must be some good drugs because you are out of your mind. I could afford that price, but that doesn't mean I would pay that.

I dropped my friend off at her place, and as I was walking up the alleyway stairwell, I heard something behind me and looked back (Dad, you would be proud of me since you always hated alleys), and I saw a nice-looking fellow. He continued past me, and we went separate ways at the top of the steps, and then he shouted back, "Excuse me, do you speak English?" I thought he was going to ask me for directions. I'd been there for a month, so I felt like I had the lay of the land, but instead, he asked, "Can I take some photos of you?"

Fresh from the beach and playing hooky from our seminar so I could attend my friend's daughter's birthday, I was without makeup, had a cold, and had just given my friend a massage. Covered in a mix of bug spray, suntan lotion (for my friend's massage), sand, and probably boogers, I was not feeling the most model-esque, by any means.

I was skeptical too, of course, (don't worry, Dad), but he whipped out his camera and showed me the photos he'd taken. I pronounced him legit and quite talented, so I let him take some pictures of me. I figured that since I was on vacation, why not?

He showed the photos to me afterward, and they were pretty good considering the hot mess of a model he was working with. I said, "It's too bad that I look like this right now as it would be nice to get some nicer photos after a shower and hair brushed and makeup so I can feel like a part of society." I asked him what his week looked like, and he said he was leaving for Colombia the next morning at 7:00 AM.

(*Wa wa wa*—insert depressing music.)

Shepreneur

It was my friend's last night in Croatia too, so we were all going for dinner an hour and a half from then, so I said, "How about I have a shower and brush my hair and meet you back here in thirty minutes and we'll have an hour to do photos?" He agreed, so I met him thirty minutes later and ended up being an hour late for dinner.

There are so many amazing humans in the world if you're open to meeting them. I know some people who think that everyone is out to get them or others, or that people have ulterior motives. If you believe that, it will keep aligning with you and will propel and snowball that cycle of thoughts and outcomes; alternatively, if you are open to the good in people, there's an excellent chance and a much higher probability that's all that you will be surrounded by.

Be realistic.

In Tuscany, my girlfriend and I were looking for things to do and saw these adorable Fiat cars, the teeny-weeny kind that a Honda Civic would plow over. Keep in mind that at home, I have a Range Rover that's quite large.

We were considering taking a tour, which consisted of a one-hour drive, a two-hour wine tour, and then a drive back. However, on tour, you would drive in a row with other people, and the rebel in me didn't want to be in a line like kids holding onto a string in preschool.

I wanted to drive where I wanted to go, so we rented a bubble-gum-pink 1964 Fiat for three days. The car was uber adorable, but my two massive sixty-pound bags did not fit, let alone my carry on or any of her bags.

Luckily, they had a little shed where you picked up the cars, so we took our toiletries and a couple of outfits we could stuff around us in the car, and off we went. At first, it was all fun and dandy; we giggled and laughed a lot because it was quite like a circus car. I hadn't driven standard in a while, so that was fun. The horn was a pipsqueak as expected, and the scenery was breathtaking.

(Insert the reality of the car.)

The rental agent advised us to stop the car every hour for fifteen minutes. Why? We learned it was because smoke started coming up from the gear shift, and it felt like it was on fire. Our cell phone flashlights were brighter than the high beams, which wasn't so great at night on the rolling hills, and a washing machine probably has more horsepower than that car.

Of course, there was no phone charger in a 1964 car. We needed GPS to find our Airbnb, and when my phone died, we had to sit at a gas station for two hours charging my phone. No one around us spoke English, so to communicate that we wanted to plug into a converter was challenging to convey. Oh, and if Google maps say it would be an hour to the Leaning Tower of Pisa or the beautiful coast of Cinque Terre, it would be more like four to five and half hours with those wheels.

The thought of the bubble-gum-pink Fiat was good, but the functionality, not so much.

We did stay at an Airbnb that had an incredible 360-degree view, but I was more in heaven because the owner had six massive dogs! I have no idea what kind they were, but they probably weighed 130 to 160 pounds each. I had just lost my handsome dog, Floyd, so I didn't care where we were in the world, but I was getting puppy love, so I was happy. Too bad one wouldn't have fit in our car to take back home with us.

You're never too old to learn something new.

I loved spending the New Year's holidays in Berlin. I loved how sexually free they were, and there seemed to be no judgments, and it was so open. We Ubered around from nine every night to about eleven each morning, going from nightclub to nightclub, taking in all the wild costumes, music, and extravaganzas that the wonderful city had to offer. Then we'd sleep all day. I've never seen a place shoot off fireworks for so long.

I also loved their clothes and wild styles. I saw someone with a pink mohawk and a big, furry jacket in lime green (I love me a fake fur-coloured jacket) and pink army pants and then some crazy purple platforms. It was just the norm. I love their out-there anything-goes style.

About my dog Floyd's passing, while in Norway, they had a northern lights viewing tour where we got to go dogsledding. I'd seen the northern lights before in Iceland, so I didn't care so much, but being around 360 or so dogs was my idea of heaven. I honestly don't think I have ever been so excited in my life and couldn't wait to get there.

They were going on and on about the lights, and much like a kid in a candy store, I was nodding and thinking, *Yes, but when do we get to see the dogs?* It was a fun night of bumps and turns on the dogsleds. The dogs would howl any time we stopped to wait for the other teams to catch up because they just wanted to run. I liked visiting them, and it was cute to see their names on the doghouses.

(Of note, one dog was named Tinder.)

My dad and stepmom watched two documentaries about Bhutan, Anthony Bourdain's *Parts Unknown*, and *The Wonder List with Bill Weir*. Since I like to travel, the three of us decided to visit Bhutan. There were some good, paved roads and some other cliffside afraid-you-will-fall-off roads.

My stepmom said after the first day, "I'm staying here. I'm not going any farther. You guys go ahead." The roads scared her so much, plus we also got stopped two or three times for landslides down the sides of the mountains, which would take hours to get back to normal, but it's all a part of the journey, right?

After working through some of her traumatic childhood memories that had arisen, we were able to move forward and continue our journey. We ended up also being in Nepal and climbing 3,210 metres (i.e., 10,531 feet up Poonhill). It was an incredible release and experience at the top with my seventy-three-year-old stepmother—you're never too old!

Help where you can along the way.

I try to give back wherever I can (except when I'm bartering, that is). I'm not the most successful realtor in my area, but I'm in the top percentile, so we don't sell the most homes. However, yesterday, we were voted the number 1 pick by the public, which felt amazing. Still, I spend more on parties for my clients in a month than other realtors spend in a year just because I love throwing parties. We all know life is short, so why not have fun while we're here?

As I may have mentioned, I love decorating, and I wanted to do something different, so I advertised a contest for a free boy and girl room makeover. They didn't have to be my clients, and I preferred if they weren't.

I didn't tell the public this, but I picked the little boy because he was severely bullied, yet he'd still help the boys in class who were beating him up and telling him he'd be better off dead.

When he grew his hair long to donate to cancer for his grandma, the bullies would call him a girl and drag him around by his hair. His mom asked, "Do you tell them why you're growing your hair out?" He said, "No. I want them to like me for me, not for something I'm doing."(Insert me crying.)

He was one of four children, and the family lived in a tiny house with no basement. I had a custom loft bed made for him with pegs as ladder steps to the top because he loves BMX biking. He also wanted green paint, which is not a colour I would ever paint a room, but I did it for him. I covered the room in BMX posters.

I also bought him sweaters, T-shirts, hats, custom Vans, a desk, a big dresser that looked like lockers, light fixtures, a closet organizer, and so forth.

Then I asked permission from his parents to have a half-pipe made and installed outside so he could practice his tricks. After he saw his room at the big reveal, I told him that I wanted to see his BMX bike tricks, so we went outside for him to show his family and myself, and when he saw that half-pipe, it was amazing! Moments like these give me chills, and that's why I do what I do.

The little girl I chose for the room makeover gave to charity all the time. She was always asking where she could donate her piggy bank money or where she could donate her clothes and toys to deserving kids. She also had a wish jar for the world where she would write something every day and put it in the jar.

Her room was made over in pink that she picked, and I had a two-level bed made for her. One level was for sleeping, and the other level was a karaoke stage (she was quite the performer), which doubled as a fort underneath. She also got new bedding, a couch under her bed, dresser, lighting, curtains, a karaoke machine, closet organizer, and so forth. I plan to do more makeovers, but next time, I am going to remake a different room, like a bathroom or a kitchen.

I also throw two massive parties a year—one for kids and one for adults—and a multitude of little ones. Each party is different. One time, it was at an ice skating rink where I had Cirque du Soleil performers over the top while people skated below, massage therapists giving massages, and a game show with prizes, build-a-bear, face painting, and so forth.

Another time, it was at a snow tubing place with tubing and sumo wrestling. Another year, it was a trampoline party at one of those indoor places with foam pits. I held one at a petting zoo where I had a firetruck, and they lit things on fire and let the kids, with the help of the fireman, put it out. I had Elsa and Anna from *Frozen* and the snowman, Olaf, at another party. But the weather wasn't cooperating, and since I spent so much money on these days, I moved the parties inside from then on.

The inside events are always at a recreation centre arena. I do different things each time, but there are typically ten to fifteen significant things, such as an obstacle course, a maze, a mechanical bull, a zip line, rock climbing, laser tag, and animals (one year, we had a skunk and kangaroo, snakes, etc.).

There might be wipeout games, magicians, Cirque du Soleil performers, mimes, people on stilts, inflatable slides, or those giant clear balls like hamsters go in but for people. They also always have food, healthy and junky, and then will have an assortment of face painting, henna, hair feathers, glitter tattoos, nail painting, and so forth.

At the end of September, I throw the adult party, which is like a wedding with a DJ, dinner, dancing, open bar, free cab rides home, and prizes. Sometimes I'll have bobbleheads made for them, or hire a psychic to read tarot cards, or a money vault. I also have something outside for when they're on route home like a funnel cake truck or crepe truck, or beaver tails, or poutine, or some kind of late-night dessert. Guests are allowed to bring whoever they want, but I only invite my clients, not everyone in the city where I live.

Then we started to hold smaller parties as the children's party is usually five hundred people on the norm, and the drinking parties have around three hundred guests. Some people have known me for a long time, and they said that the parties were too big, and they didn't get to talk to me, or they didn't like crowds or didn't drink. So I started throwing smaller parties for around thirty to sixty people, and we do little craft afternoons on Sundays.

We have done a macrame day, a painted potted plant party, etc. These parties have food but no booze. We also do lunch-and-learn days that are more real estate workshop related, and I will pick a topic such as Airbnb or Terrible Tenants. I speak, as well as have guest speakers, to share insight on what to avoid and what to do, etc.

One final way I give back is I have never sued any one of the people who have screwed me over financially, even if it's over $100,000. While that isn't necessarily giving, it helps in a way to let the debt go. I also give to charities and thoroughly enjoy that because not everyone can do so. I feel blessed to be able to donate.

Chapter 7

Gratitude

Live a Life of No Regrets

Forgiveness is underrated and super valuable.

We all have people in our lives that force us to confront our ability to forgive. Do you hang on to resentments, anger, and stale feelings? Are you stuck in the past, thinking about all the wrongs done to you? Or do you let that shit go and get back to doing you?

You know what I'm going to recommend.

Some of the things that happen to us require significant forgiveness on our part, even if there's been no apologies, acceptance, or resolution on the other person's part.

Remember when I told you that I watched all those people on the course stage in their eighties crying about past hurts? Many of them had missed the opportunity to forgive others while they were still alive. Instead, they had to write letters and read them aloud to the group or have somebody else act as a stand-in for the other person.

I didn't want to forgive the dead while I still had time to have those conversations in real-time.

Shepreneur

It wasn't easy to forgive the realtor friend of the family who had been inappropriate with me when I was young. But I had to forgive him for *me*. Although he lied saying he thought I was older, and now perhaps has a brain injury and doesn't honestly remember the incident at all, I had to forgive him and move on. Holding on to that anger and discomfort would have only hurt me and not done me or those around me any good.

I kept two diaries while growing up, one real and one fake. The fake one had a few entries in it, but it was just to throw my mom and stepdad off course. My actual diary was where I detailed all the typical kid stuff such as crushes and first kisses. I thought I was such a clever kid to have the decoy diary. One day, my mom said, "One of your diaries has a lot of stuff in it, but the other one not so much."

I was mortified that she knew I had two diaries and that she had read all my private things, so I went snooping in her room the next time she was at work. Since my mom and stepdad worked twelve-hour shifts, not counting travel, I was often at home alone for long periods.

To my surprise, I found that my mom kept a diary as well, so I parked myself on her bed and started to read. She wrote that she didn't know what to do with me, say to me, or which games to play with me. She said that she was often at a loss for words with a child. This made sense to me, as I could feel that tension when I was growing up.

When Omi, my favourite grandparent, passed away from a brain tumor, she left me her old VW Jetta—the only thing of value she had. My stepdad said to avoid having it sit in our driveway until I turned sixteen, that they would keep it at his friend's house until I was old enough to drive.

As I got closer to my sixteenth birthday, I kept inquiring about that old car but was always ignored, and the subject was changed. Eventually, they said that it was a privilege to have a car, and since it wasn't worth any money, they had scrapped it. Later, I learned that it was sold. This was the same year I moved out.

Although it was easy to be upset when I was younger, as an adult, I can look back and see how things were challenging for my mom. She was raised by a strict German man who didn't let her listen to music or play games and was very into religion. She rebelled against him and his rules, fell in love with a boy, got pregnant, and had a child in high school in the early '70s. The child was removed from her, even though she wanted to keep her. However, my grandparents had just divorced, and my grandma said they couldn't even afford the apartment they had—let alone another mouth to feed.

My mom married my father in university, and seven years later, they had me. Her tailbone was broken during my birth because my head was so big, as I weighed almost ten pounds. Then I turned out to be a colicky baby. By the time I was a toddler, my mom was single again and forced to live with friends and go on assistance from the government. She went back to school, got a nursing job, met my stepfather, and then her mom died, and shortly after, her child moved out. I'm condensing her story, but it hasn't been all rainbows and sunshine for her.

Why do I tell you all this? Because we all have our stories, everyone we know and love has their stories. I know that my mom did the very best she could for me at that time, and I do love her dearly.

Sometimes, you need time and space before you can understand a person. Then it becomes easier to forgive, which is the first step to living your life with no regrets. If you're carrying around the burden of shame and blame, it's kind of tough to be free, which brings me to my next point.

Pay attention to who you give your time to and what they are saying as well as what you are telling yourself.

Because I don't like shame, I never say, "I'm bad or not worthy or a failure because I did so many stupid things." Of course, I've done stupid things.

I mean, who hasn't?

But I prefer positive self-affirmation over the shame-and-blame game. If you're struggling with your past actions and choices, decide that today is the day you change. Just as we need to forgive others, so do we need to forgive ourselves to live a life of no regrets.

Start by doing one thing per day that will make you a better version of yourself. Once you have one thing a day down, move up to two things a day, then three. We all have lives, jobs, family, responsibility, partners, and so forth, so it's not like you can just be a goal-conquering machine all day every day. Well, you could, but there would be consequences to pay.

For most of us, there are careers and kids to run to sports practice, or you may need to be there for a friend or family member going through a hard time. Taking on three new challenges a day is manageable.

Even if you're just having a bad day, change your pattern. Listen to some music that made you happy when you were younger. Do some physical activity. It doesn't need to be a two-hour gym session, but maybe just get up from the couch and get moving. Or listen to a motivational show on YouTube or watch a funny *America's Got Talent*.

Yes, these are things that I do!

Change up your current state, so you don't go down the drain or rabbit hole of stress, angst, and worry.

Pay attention to the people around you and what they say to you. For example, what if you hear

- ❑ you're old;
- ❑ you'll never be like them;
- ❑ you're not pretty or smart enough to run in that circle;
- ❑ you shouldn't wear those clothes because they're too provocative, or you don't have the body for them; and
- ❑ you don't deserve anything.

Don't listen to all that nonsense! Look yourself in the eyes and know that you are your cheerleader, pep squad, coach, and lifeline. Examples of things you could say to yourself include these:

"I" statements

- ☐ I love you.
- ☐ I am a positive person.
- ☐ I am healthy.
- ☐ I am a miracle.
- ☐ I am optimistic.
- ☐ I do not have to prove myself to anyone.
- ☐ I can reach any goal I set for myself.
- ☐ I say *yes* to life.
- ☐ I am beautiful.
- ☐ I am present.
- ☐ I let go of everything that does not serve me.
- ☐ I am my own superhero.
- ☐ I deserve only goodness.
- ☐ I am the only one who can stop me.
- ☐ I am world-conquering.
- ☐ I am worthy.
- ☐ I can do anything.
- ☐ I let go.
- ☐ I am determined.
- ☐ I forgive myself.
- ☐ I love everything I see in me.
- ☐ I have all I need.
- ☐ I treat each day as the gift that it is.
- ☐ I am prosperous.
- ☐ I do not give up.
- ☐ I am kind.
- ☐ I am respectful and respected.
- ☐ I am strong.
- ☐ I am healing.
- ☐ I do not compare myself to anyone else.
- ☐ I am myself, and I shine brightly.
- ☐ I deserve the best.
- ☐ I trust and follow my intuition.
- ☐ I am powerful.
- ☐ I am in purposeful relationships (whether those be friendships or intimates).
- ☐ I am desirable.
- ☐ I am smart.
- ☐ I am a goal-crushing machine.
- ☐ I am giving.
- ☐ I am looked up to.
- ☐ I am unstoppable.
- ☐ I am fearless.
- ☐ I am relentless.
- ☐ I am unique.
- ☐ I am sexy.
- ☐ I am indestructible.

- ❑ I am balanced.
- ❑ I am choosing and not waiting to be chosen.
- ❑ I am loved.
- ❑ I am understanding.
- ❑ I am a fighter.
- ❑ I am filled with energy.
- ❑ I honour who I am.
- ❑ I am confident.
- ❑ I am at peace with myself.
- ❑ I create my reality.
- ❑ I am willing to change.
- ❑ I love life.
- ❑ I am a magnet that attracts abundance.
- ❑ I am aware of my worth.
- ❑ I am limitless.
- ❑ I am gorgeous.
- ❑ I am talented.
- ❑ I envision a beautiful future and live it every day.
- ❑ I am forgiving and loving.
- ❑ I am superior to toxic thoughts and actions.
- ❑ I am powerful.
- ❑ I am free from drama.
- ❑ I am in harmony.
- ❑ I love where I reside.
- ❑ I am perfect as I am.
- ❑ I am humble.
- ❑ I trust my instincts.
- ❑ I am funny.
- ❑ I am wealthy.
- ❑ I am graceful.
- ❑ I vibrate with love.
- ❑ I am divine.
- ❑ I love learning.
- ❑ I am purpose.
- ❑ I am better and better with each passing day.
- ❑ I am motivated.
- ❑ I am the master of my life.
- ❑ I do not feel sorry for myself.
- ❑ I overcome hurdles and move forward.
- ❑ I am genuine.
- ❑ I do not judge.
- ❑ I am just beginning this incredible journey.
- ❑ I am accepting of everything that has happened and will happen in my life.
- ❑ I love myself fully and without exception.

Shepreneur

"You" statements

- You got this.
- You are surrounded by infinite possibilities.
- You have all the universe's beauty within you.
- You are always inspired and taking action.
- You are confident.
- You share your inner peace with others.
- You are brave and going after your dreams.
- You are fearless.
- You are inspirational.
- You are talented.
- You are happy, and it exudes from you.
- You are amazing.
- You are living an amazing life, and it only continues to get better.
- You are healthy in mind, body, and soul.
- You are forgiving.
- You are following your dreams.
- You are surrounded by prosperity and good people.
- You are more than enough.
- You are succeeding.
- You are indestructible.
- You are courageous.
- You are in alignment.
- You are marvelous and surrounded by love.
- You are always positive.
- You are adventurous.
- You are making a difference.
- You are in charge of your destiny and create it with beauty and zest.
- You are beautiful.
- You peacefully remove yourself from situations that do not serve you.
- You learn from your past experiences.
- You are giving.
- You are full of love.
- You are brave.
- You are kind.
- You are brilliant.
- You are at peace.
- You are grateful.
- You are in control.
- You choose your mind's and life's content.

- [ ] You rock.
- [ ] You are enough.
- [ ] You are patient.
- [ ] You are complete.
- [ ] You are a creator.
- [ ] You are using your full potential.
- [ ] You are magic.
- [ ] You are admired.
- [ ] You are ready for any challenges.
- [ ] You impress me every day.
- [ ] You are courageous.
- [ ] You are my hero.
- [ ] You are safe.
- [ ] You are giving.
- [ ] You make the right choices.
- [ ] You are not limited by old patterns.
- [ ] You are in harmony.
- [ ] You can do anything you set your mind to.
- [ ] You are a visionary.
- [ ] You are calm.
- [ ] You are always focusing on the good.
- [ ] You matter.
- [ ] You are kicking ass.
- [ ] You are surrounded by people living their life on the next level.
- [ ] You are important.
- [ ] You create your own success.
- [ ] You are unbeatable.
- [ ] You are in perfect health.
- [ ] You can say no when you need to.
- [ ] You are on fire.
- [ ] You are in control of all your actions and thoughts.
- [ ] You can achieve anything you want.
- [ ] You are a positive example.
- [ ] You are productive.
- [ ] You attract abundance in your life.
- [ ] You can do anything you set your mind to.

Just as you pay attention to what you put in your body, you should pay attention to what you allow in your mind.

Evaluate your thought patterns:

- ❑ Who are you?
- ❑ What do you stand for?
- ❑ Do you stand for what you want?
- ❑ If not, how do you need to act to align yourself with your desires?

You can complain, or you can progress. Stop making excuses, and take action! Move forward. Be a better version of yourself every day. At first, it may be harder than taking the lazy way out, but believe me, it's such a more fulfilling world.

Stop trying to keep up with others—who cares where they are in life?

I should probably move this section to the front of the book. After all, we're living in a social media–driven world now. It's kind of hard to avoid being inundated with the lives and success and money and partners and kids and pets of others.

What if you aren't where you want to be?

What if you aren't where they are?

Scroll through your social media, and you see what everyone else on any other page sees. Perfect hair and makeup. Cute, perfect children. Adorable pets. That trip your friend was given "just because he loves me." That delicious meal someone cooked. The anniversary photo celebrating X years, "Love you, babe!"

You know…*#blessed.*

Well, trying to level the playing field to where they are only takes you backward. You shouldn't care where others are in life or what they post on social media. You shouldn't care what other people think about *you* either.

It's *your* life, not theirs.

You can't make everyone happy, so why not make yourself happy and do what's in your heart and soul? Think about what lights you up and makes you happy. Are you doing this regularly? How can you do more of it?

When you feel regret, find yourself unable to forgive others, feel bad about yourself, or compare yourself to someone else, *stop*.

Change your mindset to something positive and kick the nasty stuff out of your brain. You're the gatekeeper to your thoughts, and yes, you do have that kind of power. If you consider that your thoughts become your habits, and then your habits become your routines, you know how vital a healthy thought pattern is.

If you have bad thoughts, that turns to bad routines, and they can poison your dreams, relationships, and life!

Keep your thoughts clean. If you do catch a lousy thought (we all have them), address it right away and move on to something more healthy. Say to yourself, "I don't have time for you," or

"Nope, I don't think so—we may have been toxic friends in the past, but we're done."

If it's just a quick thought, get rid of it, but if it's a recurring story, you'll need to do some digging and get to the bottom of its origin. Then you and others involved in this story and scenario can be free. While it may not be holding you back from enjoying every day, perhaps it will help you and others to banish it.

We all know where those bad feelings get us, which is nowhere good. Design your life for your ultimate happiness.

Friends are the family you choose.

If you have a fantastic circle of friends but maybe are not as close to your family, I don't judge. As long as you're supported and have healthy routines together and encourage each other, then more power to you.

As we know, misery loves company. So if you a have miserable company, then it's time to find a new company if you want to change and live a better life—and not one of mediocrity.

My grandma always had funny greetings on her answering machine, and once, it said something along the lines of "Hi, you've reached Irene. I've made some changes in my life, please leave a message, if I don't call you back, you're one of them."

It's funny, but it's true: sometimes you have to make those hard choices to preserve your sanity and get to another level of growth.

Kristin Cripps

I don't ever want to have regrets. I want to learn from everything. I don't care what people think of me, and I never have. I've always done what I've wanted to do, regardless of what anyone else thinks about it.

(Oh wait, except for when I didn't become a landlord for eight years because I was listening to the advice of others. And who did that benefit? Certainly not me.)

I am a very spur-of-the-moment person. If something comes to my mind, such as a place I want to visit, I look it up, look up my schedule, then book it. I don't want to say, "Perhaps in twenty years, I will make it there."

For example, if the person I am dating and I are talking about going someplace, later that night, I could surprise them by making all the travel arrangements and buying the tickets for us to leave in the next few days. I don't wait to do the things I want to do, but I do them as quickly as I can. I also don't like being told by the media or society to buy gifts on Valentine's Day, birthdays, etc. I prefer random acts of kindness.

When I do something dumb, I might think, "Oh boy, that was stupid," but I won't regret it or shame myself. I won't think, "You dated that person, and you shouldn't have," or "You made that mistake," or "You lost $20,000."

I think, "That's okay. The next time I find myself in the same situation, I will remember this and make better decisions, so I'm not in the same boat again."

Shepreneur

Sometimes it might take a few more slaps in the face before I get it into my head, but hopefully, it only takes one. But I'd never ever beat myself up, even if it did take a few times to learn a lesson. I've always been like that. I don't know why. I think it's because I've always been too busy to worry about things. I had no time before moving onto the next thing. It's not like, "It's my party, and I'll cry if I want to."

I'm not crying: I have shit I have to do, and I'm on to the next thing in my life.

Sometimes it takes a few tries (believe me).

I dated somebody, and he was the spitting image of somebody I dated prior—only worse. I asked myself what in the world I was doing because I'd changed so much in that time to realize then that it was the same type of person (but a worse version). It was the same thing, money-wise, with both people.

With the first person, I lost $35,000 in a year and a half. With the last person, I lost $45,000 in three weeks. I want to help people, but I have learned that I need to help them from afar, not from so close. And I don't need to date them to help them, and I don't need to enable them either.

Sometimes I'm too trusting with people.

Once I realized what I had gotten myself into *again*, I knew I needed to end the relationship, but I was a bit mad at myself for letting that happen when I'd done so much work and changed so much. The first relationship lasted for a while, but the second time, I came to my senses after noticing the patterns after three weeks and cut the ties.

(There will be no "third time's the charm" in this sequence.)

Before I left for vacation, my contractor said he was sleeping in his car and needed a place, so I let him move into one of my rentals, which happened to be two doors away from me. I allowed him to stay without paying rent, and I furnished the place since he had always been such a good contractor, and I had tons of staging extras. I saw a softer kindness to him buried under a lot of hurt and fear and wanted to help him get back on his feet.

When I was out of town, he said, "I need $10,000 to do Rosenfeld. I need $5,000 to do Longboat. I need $6,000 to start Fraserburg," and so on and so on. Then, when I got back from my trip, I saw that nothing had been done or purchased even though I'd sent him all the money he'd requested.

So it's not like I don't make mistakes.

But maybe the difference between me and some others might be the way I handle myself if I feel like I'm in a bit of a rut or having an off day. For example, when I have a terrible day, I'll go to the gym and work hard, especially on the punching bag. Sometimes I'll cry when I'm at the gym. People might think I'm a weirdo, and I don't care. I'll try and blend my tears into my sweat.

Or I'll put something on YouTube, and I'll start doing squats or some other form of exercise to change my mood. Other people might smoke, but luckily for me, I despise cigarettes, so I find something good for my body.

Shepreneur

I don't want to be around people, in relationships, or have friendships that are not raising me or allowing me to encourage them to go after their dreams. I think we've all dated the wrong person, and we think we learn our lesson but find ourselves in the same scenario down the road and think we're backtracking. Then we beat ourselves up.

Or maybe we say or do something which isn't necessarily the higher or classier road and blame it on the booze or the drugs, but deep down, we know it wasn't because of the substance. Maybe someone's cheated on a loved one or stole something or said something that they didn't mean.

I think we tend to remember things more than others. Most people won't remember that thing you did, and you've been beating yourself up for over five years now. I think being straight up with people is the easiest and best way. I've been told that I don't have a filter, but why have one?

Life is too short, and if you want to know something or say something, then go for it. But I do believe in what most of our parents taught us back in the day: if you don't have anything nice to say, then don't say anything at all.

Why be nasty? It's not pleasant.

Chapter 8

Envisioning

Right Here, Right Now

Whatever you think you can have, you will have.

I visited a medium a few years back, and she asked, "Are you here to talk to anyone from the other side?"

When I said no, she said, "Good—because there's no one here to talk to you." I laughed, and she asked, "Well, then why are you here?"

I said, "I'm an open person."

She said, "It doesn't seem like it. Once a month, I get someone who's hard to read, and today, that person is you."

I apologised and closed my eyes and tried to be as calm as possible. Eventually, the woman dove into the current place where I was and said I had come to see her for an answer, which was true. She confirmed that I was contemplating a particular action.

She said, "You're thinking about getting back with your ex." I waited in suspense, as she was absolutely right. "If you do, you will have nothing left in three years."

Shepreneur

It turned out that three years was precisely how long my lawyer said we had to be together before I would have to split everything I owned with my ex, plus pay spousal and other supports.

That's what I came to find out. Thank you. Next!

We're all human; no one has superpowers.

(Well, except for that psychic medium, who was right on the nose.)

But seriously, no one can leap over buildings or shoot fire or webs out of their hands as superheroes do.

While we may not have superpowers, we do, however, have other gifts, and many people don't take the time to develop them; they remain stuck in their shit. Why not choose to be whatever you desire and then make it happen? After all, you have the power! There's no reason for not doing so, besides those excuses you make up in your head, and that's just your brain giving you fear.

Take fear as you desire, but don't take it as you have in the past. Instead, why not try one of these definitions on for size?

- ❑ FEAR: Feeling Excited And Ready
- ❑ FEAR: False Evidence Appearing Real
- ❑ FEAR: Face Everything And Rise
- ❑ FEAR: Face Everything And Rejoice

Go out and try your best!

Get your mindset in the game. Get it tuned and aligned with your goals and on your side. Only you can stand in your way, and thoughts can be the death of you. So work through them and conquer them. It's hard, but you need to break the cycle.

But how?

Always visualize.

You become what you think about most of the time. What are the thoughts you tell yourself? What are you reading? What are you listening to or streaming online? Are you planning for the future and learning what you need to know?

Make sure you are laying the foundation with healthy and not toxic thoughts, words, behaviours, or patterns.

Lots of things that I visualize in advance come true; sometimes they're small, and sometimes they're big. I told you the story earlier that my grandma used to watch me every other weekend, and we would do visualization together. She would say, "On this cloud, we're getting massages," or "On this cloud, we're with all our friends having a big barbecue."

She didn't take it into careers or anything or say, "On this cloud, you're signing your newest best-selling book." Instead, she focused on massages and music and friends. So I started learning little things about visualization with her when I was young. It doesn't have to be big things to start, but I did learn to visualize things until they happened.

Sometimes I'll do visualizations before I go to bed, and sometimes I'll do it in the morning. I like to change up my visualizations as well. Perhaps I envision a scenario where I'm a guest on *The Ellen DeGeneres Show*. I imagine her delivering her intro, and then I picture myself walking across the stage, waving at the audience, and sitting down to talk to a smiling Ellen, but staying on guard in case she does something to scare me—as she loves to scare her guests.

At other times, I'll think of warmth that starts with my forehead and goes down across my eyes, mouth, neck, and shoulders. Maybe because I was a massage therapist, I'm more in touch with energy. I'll go through my body and feel how it would feel if I was giving a million dollars to my favorite charity. Or I'll imagine that I hold a renowned event, and I'll picture the people in the stadium excited and cheering.

As I create these mental scenarios, I'll go through my body and imagine how it would feel to experience those events. If you tell yourself you're ugly and fat every day when you look in the mirror, then that becomes you. I don't watch sports on TV, but put me at a game, and I love it because I can feel the energy. I try and emulate the energy in my thoughts when I visualize, and then I feel it throughout my body. I notice that warmth and allow that good energy to spread through me.

I'll imagine my nephew or someone's child playing baseball who never does well and then see him hitting the home run that sends everybody to home base, which wins the game. I'll see him running past his teammates and straight to his mother or me, depending on the situation, feeling his energy and the excitement of the team.

Or I will picture a loved one who was in a tragic car accident, and then turns out that they are okay—and I have no idea they're alive until the doorbell rings, and they're at my door. Both these were given to me by the talented Steffani LeFevour, author of *You Are A Badass Mom: A Guide to Take Your Life, Love, and Parenting to the Next Level.*

I think of good visions and want to feel positive energy, because when I was younger, I used to think of dramatic situations. I don't want toxic, nonserving thoughts in my head. So I try my darndest to only have joyous thoughts in my head and expansive and abundant good scenarios, instead of letting my brain go to unhealthy places.

That's why I don't like being addicted to things. People are sucked into binge-watching all the latest shows. I don't like watching those programs because I don't want to fuel an unhealthy habit. I'd rather listen to podcasts, TED Talks, YouTube interviews, and motivational mantras or attend seminars.

I don't want to watch the drama of this person cheating on that person and then that person flipped the table or pulled someone's hair. I don't want and will not get addicted to those kinds of shows because they're not good for my soul, brain, or energy. I want to have intentional control of my mind, life, reactions, and output to the world. I am conscious of doing such.

Journaling.

I have a variety of techniques I use to create my reality. For example, I might say, "I am an amazing sister who is always supportive and there for my siblings."

I do *not* say, "I hope that with practice and study, I will one day be an amazing sister."

When you hope or try, you will always find excuses not to fulfill it, but when you say, "I am…," it does something in your brain, helping rewire your thoughts to align with your words. I'm not going to give you a full-blown neurology lesson, nor am I qualified to do so. But what you say and think has been shown in studies that the neurotransmitters and chemicals like dopamine and serotonin and all the good happy feeling ones are released with a positive affirmation.

Instead of saying, "I'm going to do something," or "I'm going to be a certain way," I say that I already am that way. I say, "I am a world-class speaker."

For example, "I am giving $1 million a year to my favorite charity." I say it like I'm doing it, not hoping that one day I can or *maybe* I will try next year, because this places doubt in my brain. Doubt will win any day, so I don't want any doubt in my mind or the world I have created. I write, think, speak, and visualize different scenarios, so my brain doesn't get used to things.

It's kind of like going to the gym and doing the same exercises all the time: your body will plateau and stop burning fat and building new muscle. You always need to be making changes and tweaks and approaching it from different angles, whether that be the gym or your thoughts and visualizations.

The second way I like to journal is to talk in the third person and speak as if it has already happened. An example would be,

"Jacqueline is an amazing cook. She started cooking for friends and now has a syndicated show where she teaches others all over North America how to eat healthy on a budget." (If I was Jacqueline, that is.)

For example, I recently did two interviews for a docuseries. Before I went in for the lunchtime taping, I did my usual morning routine, which includes writing in my gratitude journal and "I Am" journal. For example, I wrote something like this:

> I am knowledgeable, funny, and authentic in today's docuseries. I am seen in the two docuseries and over five hundred interviews, speaking engagements, and interviews come from the docuseries. I am meant to be here. I am clever. I am beautiful. I am grateful. I am a successful entrepreneur. I am a wealth of knowledge. I am giving to those who need my knowledge most. I am laughter, I am kindness, I am capable, I am strong.

Another technique I sometimes practice is to write a letter to my younger self. This is a super empowering practice to imagine and say to your little self what you would say to them now, such as the following:

- ❏ "You're going to be okay."
- ❏ "They don't mean it, and it has to do with their issues."
- ❏ "It's not personal."
- ❏ "I know this is shitty now, but one day, you will find true love."
- ❏ "He/she will not hurt you again."

- ❏ "You will get through this, and you are unstoppable."
- ❏ "The words he/she speaks are not true reflections of who you are or are going to become."
- ❏ "You are magnificent."
- ❏ "I believe in you."

I've also written letters to myself at an age when I was experiencing a hard time. For example, you could pick the period when your parents divorced, experienced your first heartbreak, or maybe lost a loved one or were taken advantage of. You could write:

"Dear twenty-three-year-old self, this is your thirty-seven-year-old self. I have a few things to tell you…"

It can be quite therapeutic.

Be around like-minded people.

One of my favorite techniques is to enlist your friends to share an envisioning session. Let's say you envision opening an orphanage, and you're helping two thousand children a year. Gather all your friends together, and tell them about your dream. Close your eyes while they talk about it around you as if it's already happened. They'll think of things that you might not have, and you can relax into a healthy growing environment where your dreams are instead of in a toxic environment.

For example, imagine that you are gathering to support your friend, Natalie:

"Oh, I saw Natalie on *Oprah*—she's been on her show three times this year already!"

"She's so motivational. I watch every show she's on!"

"Did you see Natalie on *Dr. Phil* when he matched her million-dollar donation to her orphanage?"

"I heard she's written a book about the orphanage and using the proceeds to open even more orphanages!"

"Her next speaking engagement sold out in less than twenty-four hours!"

Then you take turns. Your friend shares his or her vision, and the rest of you make comments. Let's say Mark wants to help kids in underdeveloped countries get the chance to be drafted and play in major league sports. Next, he closes his eyes, and we say things around him such as these:

"I saw Mark on *MarieTV*! He talked about how he opened three schools last month—one in Africa, one in Papua New Guinea, and another in Guatemala."

"Oh, I heard about Mark! I just read his number 1 best-selling book in my book club, and I heard that he's giving all the proceeds to his foundation!"

"They gave $10 million last year to help build sports domes for kids and bring in professional athletes to train them."

"He's so humble! Did you hear he has adopted four of the children?"

"I saw him on the cover of *Time* magazine, and he's going to be on *Oprah* next month, I can't wait to see him!"

"I heard he's speaking on TEDx. I'm going to try to get tickets."

"Yeah, I was at a Tony Robbins event last month, and he said he's matching whatever Mark donates in 2020!"

"There were over a thousand kids the first year alone who got drafted, and now over three-quarters of those kids have started foundations and charities as well!"

You become what you think about most of the time.

My code to my online banking was not working one day, and I kept typing my code, but it wouldn't work. Then I typed "fuckingidiots" out of frustration, and not because that was even close to my code—but it worked, so "fuckingidiots" stayed my code for over eight years.

Sounds funny, right?

But then I started thinking about how you become what you think about most of the time. I considered how many times a day I typed in "fuckingidiots." What you say and think and feel and manifest and tell yourself really happens. So saying "fuckingidiots" every time before I looked at my bank account couldn't be a wise idea. I changed my password to the amount of money I wanted to make during a particular year.

Then I achieved it.

Ah, the power of the mind and intentions!

Your homework

Now that you're almost finished with the book, I'm going to give you some homework. I want you to grab two pieces of paper.

Think about what you would do if you were retired, and you had all the money in the world. Maybe you'd see Paris, learn how to ride a unicycle, climb Mount Everest, take tango dancing lessons, run a marathon, go to Colombia for a month, learn how to cut hair, do some stand-up improv, learn how to massage, or sing opera.

Write down all those things.

On the next page, pretend you're already retired and start to fit those things into your schedule. Look into opera lessons or a massage technique class. See how much a package to Paris or Colombia costs. Find out when the next open-mic night is at the closest comedy show, and add it to your calendar.

Otherwise, if you make no plan, then life will make its own plan, whether you agree with it or not, and then almost with a snap of your fingers, eight years will pass, and you'll wonder where the time went.

Shepreneur

Imagine you have only one week to live.

Who would you see? What would you do? Would you turn off your phone and stay with your loved ones the whole time? Would you go bungee jumping? Would you tell your boss to shove it? Would you tell your high school crush even though you're now fifty that you would love to go on a date and pick up where you left off?

Now ask yourself why you're not living that life every day.

Conclusion

Carpe Diem

Don't Backburner Your Life

Remember, at the beginning of the book, when I told you that everyone is a millionaire?

Well, that makes you a millionaire, too.

Yes, you right there—the one with this book in your hand.

Real wealth in all aspects of life is not only what you find in a bank account. People find richness in a variety of ways, such as by giving to and helping others.

Look around your life, and see where you're banking it.

Your family? Your friends? Your volunteer work? Your bank accounts? Your career? Your partner? Do you have abundance in all aspects, or are you a millionaire of excuses?

Sometimes when we're looking for what's missing, we miss everything that's already there.

I see signs and often equate them to how I see people perceive life and situations. For example, recently, I saw a massive boat with one teeny tugboat pulling it from the front and another tugboat trailing behind. The teeny one in the front was pulling that big boat, which almost looked impossible, but of course, it wasn't.

I feel that the small tugboat in front represents that entrepreneur who gives it their all and makes it happen. They don't think they're too small, or in physics, their actions may not make any sense, but they still go hard after their dreams! They persevere and say, "I don't care that this doesn't seem to make sense or isn't logical: I'm going to do it anyway."

I believe that the tiny tugboat behind represents 98 percent of people who are too worried to act. They wonder, "Should I pass? No, a bigger boat might come and hit me," or "Should I try to tow him? No, I'm not strong enough," or "Should I be going this direction at all? What if it's the wrong way?"

"No way" is the wrong way.

An experience may be a detour you weren't expecting or planning, but it will still have a lesson.

If you think your day is terrible, and the world is out to get you, know that this too will pass. You can conquer it, and it will make you stronger. There's at least one lesson in it, if not more, and it's happening *for* you, not *to* you. Get out of the victim mentality, and see everything as an opportunity to grow and be a better, more superior, and improved version of yourself as much as humanly possible.

You have to start somewhere, and today might as well be your day.

Analyze your routines. If you zombie through life, you may not realize that bad habits can poison any idea, relationship, career, or life.

Do you know how they say when one door closes, another opens?

(Yeah, I know it's a cliché, but hear me out.)

A lot of people experience that first door closing and then sit in a chair in one room and wait for only that one door to open. You need to go out of the room and walk down the hall and open all the other doors—or knock or ring the bell or do something.

You can't just sit and wait—you must do!

I sold a client's house on a Tuesday night. The very next morning, he called an ambulance and had to go to the hospital. He's young, about the same age as my dad. He's not in the shape that my dad is, though. He's shorter than me and quite overweight, plus he has chronic congestive heart failure, liver failure, diabetes, and other illnesses. Or at least that's just what the nurses told me when I went to visit him, as I asked them questions while he was sleeping. They told me that he had a heart attack three years ago as well.

The reason I am ending the book with this story is that he listed his house with me because he wanted to travel. He'd never done much travelling and decided it was his time to see the world. So he sold his house, but I don't think he knew the actual severity of his health challenges and that travelling wasn't very likely in his cards.

Shepreneur

In my career, I see people who wait to sell their home until after the kids have moved out, and then they plan to go on their dream trip or buy that sailboat they've had their eye on or take that pottery class.

Why wait to go after your dreams?

We don't know when our time will be up, so don't wait—seize the days you have now because none of us are psychic to know when that last day is. (Except maybe for that one psychic who told me nobody was there to speak to me.) The rest of us have to live as if our time is limited here—because it is.

If you learned that you had minutes left before a natural disaster was going to wipe out your city, would you have any regrets in life? What would you have done if you had one more week, one more year, or five more years?

We never know when we will get that call, be it as drastic as my example or from a doctor with bad news. Maybe you'll get no call at all, and one day, your ticket will be up. What do you still want to accomplish in your life, say, try, or experience?

When it's your time to go, don't leave with tears of unfulfilled dreams and sadness. Instead, shed tears of joy and happiness, knowing that you gave it your all from start to finish, or even middle to finish, which is better than never going after it or speaking up at all.

Now might be a good time to have some fun. Take out your pen and paper, or open a blank document on your computer and write your obituary. It's not morbid—let loose!

Kristin Cripps

Here is my obituary, where I pretended that I had passed and wrote my obituary in my final year:

> Kristin Cripps passed at the peak of an orgasm at the ripe age of 108 (although you would have guessed her to be in her early fifties). Kristin was born in London, Ontario, and spent most of her life in Ontario, but she was a traveler at heart and had homes that she frequented across the globe.
>
> The true meaning of a powerhouse woman, Kristin was kicking butt up until her last day. She had a zest for life like no other, always wanting to live with the most vibrancy possible. Kristin had no children but enjoyed an army of nieces, nephews, friends, and lovers.
>
> Kristin had a multitude of businesses. She ran events all over the world that were attended by millions over the years. She also had a successful home furniture/ decor line and clothing line. Kristin was the best-selling author of over fifty books, had top-ranking podcasts, and was an international speaker at other events besides her own. She had a successful real estate brokerage, had funny real estate blooper shows on a variety of social media platforms followed by millions, ran online real estate how-to courses, and had a small city of real estate investments.
>
> However, Kristin was mostly known for her generosity. She regularly gave to her own charity, as

well as those dearest to her heart. She did thousands of room makeovers to contest winners through her free giveaways. Kristin had relaxation and work down to an art and always had a massive smile on her face. She travelled to more countries than most even know exist, laughed like there was no tomorrow, and gave life a real run for its money and lived an epic life.

Hells ya—see ya on the other side!

Now it's your turn!

Let loose and allow your dreams to run wild. Imagine every single thing you have ever wanted to do, and write it as if you've accomplished every last desire. Some things to consider include the following:

- ❑ The family, partner, and friends you cultivated
- ❑ The productive career(s) you had and all that you managed to do
- ❑ Your volunteer work and all the lives you changed as a result of your efforts
- ❑ Your travel to every country on the globe
- ❑ Perhaps you cured a disease, or two, or ten
- ❑ Solving global warming
- ❑ Ran and won a political office
- ❑ The monuments, awards, and scholarships established in your honor

- ❑ The experiences you've lived and shared
- ❑ The laughter you've enjoyed
- ❑ The dreams you went after (whether all achieved or not, at least you tried)
- ❑ The abundance you made for your life and all those you love

When you've finished, take in the deepest breath you have ever inhaled and smile it all in.

And now make it happen!

You can! You will! Watch you!

BONUS CONTENT: KRISTIN'S SHEPRENEUR MIXTAPE

Whatever obstacle I faced (depending on the year) there always seemed to be a series of "don't fuck with me" songs that empowered me

Hopefully you find this to be a fun playlist side note. I am so happy for you to go out and start living, or continue living—depending what part of your journey you are on—the most epic abundant lives humanly possible.

Say YES to your life.

Say YES to abundance.

Say YES to you and your dreams!

And say it while you're rocking out.

"Move Bitch" by Ludacris
"I Don't Fuck With You" by Big Sean
"Independent Women" by Destiny's Child
"Run The World (Girls)" by Beyoncé
"Girl On Fire" by Alicia Keys
"No Scrubs" by TLC
"Work It" by Missy Elliot
"Bodak Yellow" by Cardi B
"Started From The Bottom" by Drake
"Survivor" by Destiny's Child
"Work Bitch" by Britney Spears
"Diva" by Beyoncé

Shepreneur

"Bitch Better Have My Money" by Rihanna

"7 Rings" by Ariana Grande

"Hustlin'" by Rick Ross

"Can't Hold Us" by Mackelmore & Ryan Lewis

"Not Afraid" by Eminem

"All I Do Is Win" by DJ Khaled (feat. T-Pain, Snoop Dogg, & Rick Ross)

"Billionaire" by Travie McCoy (feat. Bruno Mars)

"Am I Wrong" by Nico and Vinz

"Good as Hell" by Lizzo

"Oh Yeah" by Foxy Brown (feat. Spragga benz)

Acknowledgments

While attending a month-long course in Croatia, I headed down some cobble-lined alleyway and steps first thing one July morning and I already had my first book half complete. It was about real estate, investing, and all of the ins and outs for investors. However, after sitting in this women's only seminar (the whole month wasn't that way, just that one class), I saw a connection between women and a void between women's thoughts and visions for themselves and what they actually took action and believed they could or deserved to achieve.

I was heartbroken. Always being a go-getter myself with a "I don't need anyone" kind of mentality, I had no problem facing any gender-based or other kinds of obstacles in my path. Instead, I saw a chance to show others how it doesn't matter what people think or say about you or where you grew up or what your past is—what truly matters is that you believe in yourself and what you fight for and move towards.

I wanted to write a book and create a platform for women to be the best versions of themselves, whether that be as the boss of a business, having the relationship of their dreams, having an amazing home life, having that hard conversation, or finally taking that leap that they were always too scared to take. I don't want any woman to die with regrets. If I can help anyone or motivate them or give them insight, then I will be content and inspired to show others what we can create together and better our world.

Shepreneur

I want to thank the amazing team at Leaders Press, namely (but not only) Alinka Rutkowska, Deborah Brannon, Marlayna Glynn, and all those who listened to my calls as a greedy friend only answering questions and not asking questions, and helped decipher my 10 page run-on sentences in Kristinese (a gibberish of my own language I often speak). You ladies are powerhouses, and I hope you and I inspire more and more women to take life and opportunity in their own hands and make magic!

Also, a special thanks to Dori Mangrum who took the shot in Chicago that ended up being on the book cover, while putting up with me and all of my outfit changes (that were in that suitcase).

Thank you to my friends, near and far, who supported me throughout the process and always do.

I love you all dearly! Live your best lives! Be the best you! Make a mark on this planet and have an utter blast doing it! <3 <3 <3

About the Author

Kristin Cripps is a prolific real estate investor and developer who's crushing it in the world of business. Although she left home at age sixteen, she was able to purchase her first property at age nineteen—becoming a millionaire before the age of thirty.

A former bartender, waitress, and massage therapist turned real estate mogul, today, Kristin is a highly sought-after international wealth creation coach, speaker, and trainer, who consistently features in the top 1 percent of property brokers in Canada.

Kristin is on a mission to show others how to acquire financial freedom and live a life of abundance and contentment through her proven real estate investment strategies and mindset reset techniques.

This unstoppable woman travels the world to share the *anyone-can-do-it* strategies she used to create massive success. She can often be found abroad, searching for inspiration in unique architectural design while fulfilling her quest for constant learning, growth, and development.

Despite the remarkable wealth she's created from a standing start, she is incredibly grounded and loves spending time with her family and amazing circle of loyal friends, colleagues, and her award-winning team at Cripps Realty.